WEAVE WANDERERS & WIGNEYS

Also by Tim King

Ecology (Thomas Nelson & Sons, 1982, 1990)
reprinted 15 times and published in Icelandic

Eight other textbooks

Numerous research papers

www.timjking.co.uk

WEAVERS, WANDERERS & WIGNEYS

*The Roller-Coaster Ride of
a Typical(?) English Family*

Tim King

with research by Heather Fiske King (née Wigney)

Lasius Press
Oxford

Lasius Press
93 Kingston Road, Oxford OX2 6RL
www.timjking.co.uk

First edition published by Lassius Press
Copyright (c) 2017 Tim King

ISBN: 978-1-910301-43-2

Edited and designed by Martin Noble Editorial
28 Abberbury Road, Iffley, Oxford OX4 4ES
martinnobleeditorial.com

Printed and bound in Great Britain by
Lightning Source UK Ltd,
Chapter House, Pitfield, Kiln Farm,
Milton Keynes MK11 3LW

CONTENTS

PREFACE

Of course, the Wigneys of Brighton were mushrooms.... They were mushrooms, springing up no one knew how or whence. But, mushroom-like, they throve and spread, until they filled a large space in men's eyes; and if wealth, magisterial dignity, political power, and fashionable position could give consequence, they possessed it in Brighton fifty years ago.

No family, indeed, in the history of this town ever rose so rapidly or so high as the Wigneys, and none ever fell more quickly or completely.

Charles Fleet (1883) *Glimpses of our Ancestors in Sussex*, 2nd edn. Lewes.

WHEN WE DREW UP in front of Newtimber Place, near Hassocks (Figure 0.1), about seven miles north of Brighton, we were amazed. Here was a grand Grade One-listed Sussex moated house, with several cottages, equestrian facilities and a garden open under the National Gardens scheme. Sydney (Viscount, then Earl) Buxton retired there after his spell as Governor of South Africa (1914–20).

Yet Heather's great (x5) uncle, William Wigney, from humble weaving origins in Yorkshire, erstwhile part-time smuggler, blanket dealer, draper, coal merchant and brewer, lived there in pomp as a country squire for eleven years in the early nineteenth century. Indeed, to prove it, the current owner later found a four-page indenture, two hundred years old, in his loft, explaining the terms on which William would rent the property. How on earth did this working-class speculator, from a background of poor weavers up north, manage to produce Brighton's first MP, a range of colourful grandchildren, and leave in his will perhaps the modern equivalent of over £20 million?

Figure 0.1: The front of Newtimber Place, near Hassocks, a sixteenth-to-seventeenth-century manor house about seven miles from Brighton, where William Wigney lived with his family and servants, *c.* 1811–25.

William's story is particularly interesting when viewed against a background of English social history – weavers migrating to and from Yorkshire, cloth trading all over Europe, religious non-conformism, smuggling, the expansion of Brighton as it became a mecca for the aristocracy, the French Revolutionary and Napoleonic Wars, universal suffrage, bank collapses, brewing and emigration.

William is certainly the central figure, because he created the dynasty whose escapades we have found so intriguing. The saga continued long after his death in 1836. Some of his descendants, particularly his son Isaac Newton Wigney MP, and Isaac's offspring, married aristocratic partners and became associated with the high life in London, elopements, murders, and financial chicanery. This initially successful group no longer exists as Wigneys. Yet, at the same time, another set of unusual and imaginative Wigneys were poverty-stricken. Some emigrated to the colonies, others became nonconformist pillars of society or factory workers. This group is thriving in the United Kingdom, Australia, Canada and the USA. Luckily, many left personal memoirs, which we have drawn on freely.

Our investigations were helped by the distinctive family name, WIGNEY, which does not appear in any of the standard dictionaries of British surnames. Several Wigneys left documents detailing the lives of themselves and their descendants. Several of William's articulate descendants became well-known. Newspapers of the eighteenth and nineteenth centuries reveal the minutiae of their lives and their court cases, sometimes in excruciating detail. Numerous books have been written about Brighton's history.

Our story mainly focuses on the years 1535–1922, and particularly on William Wigney (1756–1836) and his descendants. The story we tell is illuminated in particular by the extensive and detailed researches of Lorna Fiske Wigney (1916–2003) – working successfully without the internet – Lorna Marian Fiske Wigney (b. 1952), her sister Heather Fiske King (b. 1944) and Karen Wigney and Caylie Wigney in Australia. LMFW and HFK have commented fully on the text. Jennifer Smith, the author of *The Constables of Horley Mill*, has been particularly generous with her time, emails and quotations. Sue Berry's *Georgian Brighton* was a mine of well-documented information, and the late Pauline Virgo contributed photographs. We benefited considerably from the help and advice from librarians in the British Library, The London Metropolitan Library, The Keep at Brighton, the local studies section of the Halifax Central Library and the offices of the Genealogy Society in London. The constructive criticism of the Kingston Road book group, Oxford, was also appreciated. We hope that you will enjoy reading about this dynasty, and that your own family history is half as interesting. The family connection, of course, is that Heather King was born a Wigney.

While researching this book, and discussing this with friends, we realised that the sequence of lives may be difficult to follow. Our particular problems are that so many Wigneys are called William and George, and that there are so many overlapping generations. Thus we have inserted as Chapter 1 (pp. 12–15) four family trees mentioning the major characters and to some extent where they lived. We hope that you will find these useful.

Parts II–IV (Chapter 4 onwards) tell well-documented stories about the Wigneys in Brighton and beyond. Part I (Chapters 2 and 3) discusses where they came from and their historical roots in Yorkshire, Lancashire and weaving.

After the first person with a particular Christian name to appear chronologically – say William – we called the next one William II, the next William III, and so on. By labelling these Williams, Josephs, Georges and George Adolphuses in this way, both in the text and on the family trees, we found that it clarified the whole sequence.

Tim and Heather King
Oxford 2017

1

THE WIGNEY FAMILY TREES

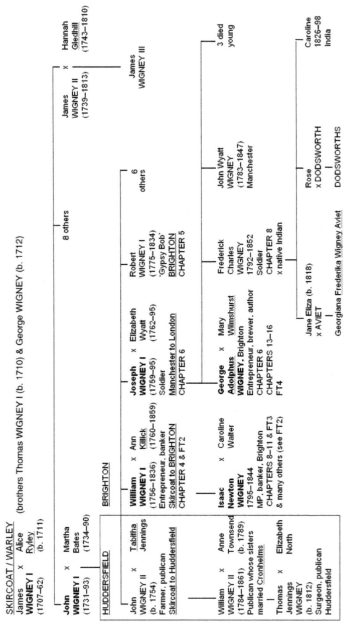

Figure 1.1: Family Tree 1 (FT1): Origins.

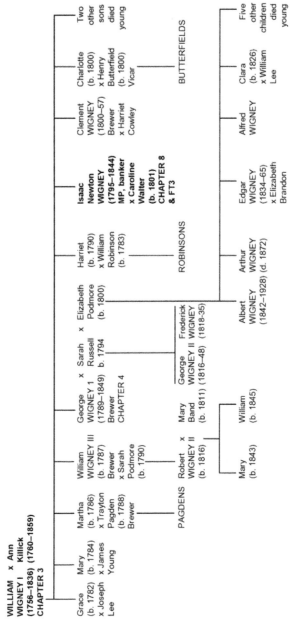

Figure 1.2: Family Tree 2 (FT2):
William Wigney I's descendants.

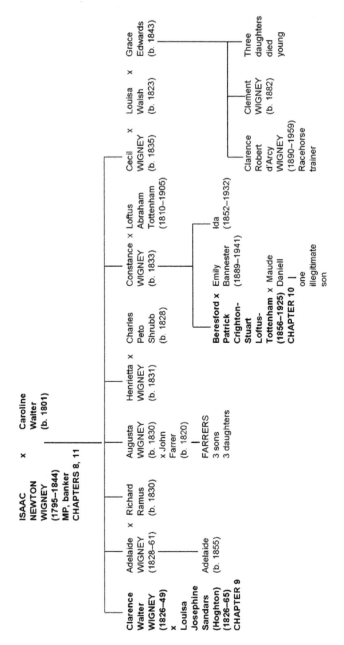

Figure 1.3: Family Tree 3 (FT3):
Isaac Newton Wigney's descendants.

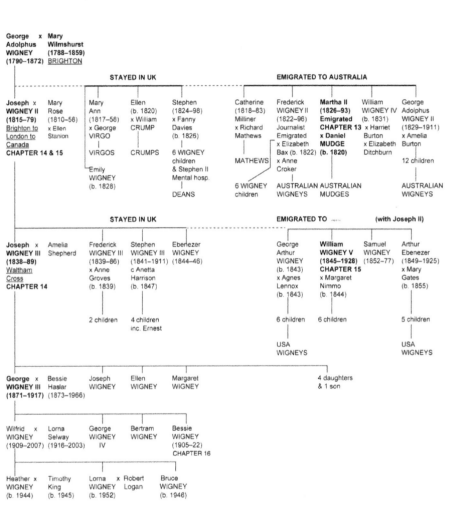

Figure 1.4: Family Tree 4 (FT4):
George Adolphus Wigney's descendants.

PART I

ORIGINS

2

BEGINNINGS

Where did the Wigneys come from?

THE WIGNEYS may ultimately have been pickled in beer, but at first they were entangled in wool.[1] Wool. Until we began this investigation into Heather's ancestry, we had no idea of its major role in Britain's economy and politics, let alone the history of the Wigney family. Even in the twelfth century, wool accounted for 90 per cent of Britain's exports.

Think of the metaphors and similes embedded in our language: 'dyed in the wool', 'home-spun wisdom', 'spun yarns', 'lost the thread', 'fabricated evidence', 'unravelled plots', 'broken bones knitted together', 'woolly arguments', 'wrapped themselves in cotton wool', 'wool pulled over their eyes', 'cloth-eared', 'fleeced', 'sheepish', 'mutton dressed as lamb', 'black sheep', 'shepherd's pie', Chancellor sits on the 'woolsack'. You can probably think of others.

Nor did we realise the striking difference in wool production between West Yorkshire and the Pennines, on the one hand, and the rest of the country on the other. In West Yorkshire, where labour and packhorse trains were cheaper than in the south, there were small landowners weaving in family concerns in groups, engaged in business, selling or distributing their finished products through a network of clothiers and merchants. This stimulated entrepreneurs, and led to many small farmers banking and giving credit. Smallholding owners owned their spinning wheels and looms, took their produce to the cloth halls and sold to merchants face to face. Down south though, large estates and farm-owners employed farmhands as serfs, on a much larger scale.

Woollen production, and the attitude of mind and social structure which enabled maximum profits to be made from it, was embedded in the culture in the West Riding of Yorkshire since the end of the fourteenth century.[2] As new techniques and machines emerged down south, such as draw looms, Saxony wheels and fly shuttles, they were adopted in the Peak District and made cloth production more efficient. Already, when Daniel Defoe[3] and his retinue came to look at the Calder Valley in 1724, on horseback and in carriages, they were staggered at what they found. As they rode from Manchester over Blackstone Edge, and then approached Halifax, they must have passed close to the Wigneys' smallholding. Whereas most of the rural population of Britain lived in poverty, around Halifax there was a high population density, no obvious hardship, and people were healthy and long-lived. They were dedicated to hard work, with a shared sense of purpose.

There, in smallholdings close together, the inhabitants wove kersies and shalloons, carding, weaving, spinning, fulling and combing. Defoe attributed their success 'in this otherwise frightful country' to copious supplies of running water and coal.

> Hardly a house standing out of a speaking distance from another ... wherever we passed any house we found a little rill or gutter of running water.... Then, as every clothier must keep a horse, perhaps two, to fetch ... home his wool and his provisions from the market, to carry his yarn to the

spinners, his manufacture to the fulling mill ... and to the
market to be sold ... so every manufacturer generally keeps
a cow or two ... for his family, and this employs the two, or
three, or four pieces of enclosed land about his house....

This 'one continued village' was whitened with cloths
decking the hillsides; 'at almost every house there is a
tenter and almost on every tenter a piece of cloth, or
kersey or shalloon'. For two or three miles in every
direction, 'look which way we would, high to the tops,
and low to the bottoms, it was all the same; innumerable
houses and tenters, and a white piece upon every tenter'.

Halifax was indeed a monster for a country parish.
'Thus this one trading, manufacturing part of the country
supports all the countries around it, and the numbers of
people settle here as bees about a hive.'[4]

Defoe then went on to Leeds, the centre of cloth
dyeing, and describes the economics of Leeds market,
where most of the cloth was disposed of in a stage-
managed event twice a week. Some was sold to London
warehouses, whence the cloth might be transported to
New York, Virginia, St Petersburg, Riga or Sweden, for
example. Some true merchants sold directly to Hamburg,
Holland, Germany and Vienna. For home consumption,

...there are for this purpose a set of travelling merchants in
Leeds, who go all over England with droves of pack horses,
and to all the fairs and market towns over the whole island
... 'tis ordinary for one of these men to carry a thousand
pounds value of cloth with them at a time.

This is how we suspect that, sixty years later, William
Wigney found Brighton.

At that stage it took six people sorting, carding,
spinning, weaving and shearing to produce one finished
but undyed kersey. Typically, the father went to market
and bought the wool; the wife and children combed,

carded and spun it; and some of the wool was put out to be spun at neighbouring properties. With the help of his sons, apprentices and journeymen, the clothier then dyed the wool, wove it, took it to the fulling mill and then to his stall in the market. He produced only one or two pieces a week. Defoe hardly saw anyone out of doors.

But if we knocked at the door of any of the master manufacturers, we presently saw a handful of lusty fellows, some at the dye-fat, some dressing the cloths, some at the loom, some one thing, some another, all hard at work.

When we buy clothes nowadays we rarely consider the sweatshops of India and the Far East in which they are produced. Equally, though, it is easy to forget the blood, toil, tears and sweat of our own ancestors, and years of improvement of the techniques which ultimately made it all possible.

This weaving industry in Lancashire and the West Riding of Yorkshire did not arise entirely by chance. By the fourteenth century the centre of cloth weaving was in the Low Countries. Most of the fleeces produced by sheep on downland in Britain were *exported* to northern France, Belgium and Holland. The cloth produced by the Flemish and Walloon weavers was then *imported* back to Britain. Edward III, realising that this was an unnecessary economic drain on Britain, imported a group of skilled Flemish weavers to England in 1358. Their arrival in Manchester, for example, is commemorated by a set of murals by Ford Maddox Brown in Manchester Town Hall. By the time the persecuted Protestant weavers from Flanders, Holland and Germany were flooding into Britain and were being welcomed for their skills, the British weaving industry was very well-established. Waves of Huguenot refugees augmented the weaving industries around Spitalfields in London, and in Norwich.

Many were nonconformists, Quakers, Baptists, Unitarians or Presbyterians.

It was into this cloth-producing and commercial environment that our main protagonist, William Wigney[5] was born in 1756, near Sowerby Bridge, close to Halifax, Yorkshire, in the Calder Valley. But where did the Wigneys originally come from?

In Belgium, there is a town called Wigny and tens of individuals on Facebook with that surname. An alternative possibility is that the name is derived from de Vigny, perhaps Huguenot wine growers fleeing religious persecution. For example, Jean de la Vigne (b. 1540, found in Valenciennes, France, 1585 and in Antwerp in 1622, died in Amsterdam)[6] was a Protestant reverend who had three sons and a daughter. Because of the weaving and dissenting background of William's parents and grandparents, his ancestors were probably emigrating weavers, perhaps Walloons. Indeed, around 1567

> the first Duke of Ormonde … established 500 Walloon immigrants at Chapel Izod, in Kilkenny, Ireland, under Colonel Richard Lawrence. He also settled large colonies of Walloons at Clonmell, Kilkenny and Carrick-on-Suir, where they established, and for some time carried on, the manufacture of woollen cloths.[7]

There are a couple of Wigneys recorded from Kirkham, Lancashire, between Manchester and the Irish Sea, in 1560–63.[8] Just before that date some persecuted Protestant Walloon weavers established colonies on the northwest coast of Ireland. It is possible that some of them travelled from Ireland to the Lancashire coast.

There are at least ten seventeenth-century records from the Church of the Latter Day Saints for Wigneys in Calderdale and the West Riding of Yorkshire. The earliest traceable individual likely to be closely related to the current

British Wigneys was Mary Wigney (1672–1746) who married John Leech (1672–1746) and had six children.[9]

Genetic analyses (see Figure 2.1) are consistent with the idea that the Walloon weaving area in the Low Countries might have been where the Wigneys came from. They match a group of current Germans.[10,11]

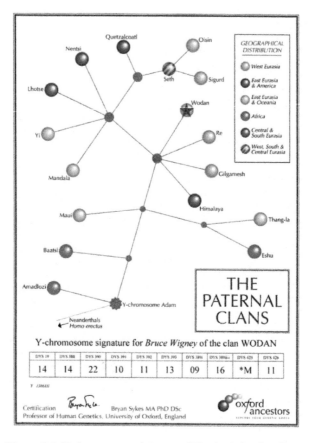

Figure 2.1: Y chromosome signature of Heather's brother, Bruce Wigney.[10,11] Clan Wodan, to which he belongs, is widespread but ultimately probably originated in the Ukraine.

There is a more prosaic possible explanation for the appearance of the Wigneys in the West Riding, which is that some lusty young fellow called Wignall crossed the Pennines, became apprenticed to a clothing trade, and began to be called Wigney. The Wignalls were abundant in the Lancashire cotton trade and, like the Wigneys, lived at Kirkham in the sixteenth century.[12] One feature of the Yorkshire dialect is that they tended to leave the final –ll off names when they spoke them. So Wignall might have become Wigna in Yorkshire. When recording births, christenings, marriages and deaths, parish clerks, sometimes responding to dictation, seem to have adopted a variety of spellings. We have seen Wignoye, Wignowe, Wygnowe, Wigno, Wigne, Wignoe, Wiggnay,Wignay, Wignigs, Wygnall, Wignell, Wignoll, Wignalghe, Wignayle, Weigny, Vignee and Vegni. It is striking that amongst the surnames of immigrants from the Low Countries to Manchester, Spitalfields, Norwich and Ireland we have been unable to find de Vigne or Wigny; but we must bear in mind that Wigny in Belgium is a small insignificant place and that there are at least six Lancashire Wignys, without the letter e, between 1672 and 1804.[13]

Halifax property

What are the secrets of social and financial success? Intelligence, a fertile imagination, a good education, determination and the capacity for hard work are perhaps desirable. Quite apart from these attributes, the Wigney men, with peripatetic tendencies, began to demonstrate a remarkable capacity for being in the right place at the right time, and for marrying women from families well-established in the local area. This stood them in good stead for generations and powered their climb up the social ladder. Was it luck, or was it judgment? Until we began this book, we had taken weaving, and the skills required, for granted. Yet every civilised human needs clothes and the skills of cloth production were specialised and localised. The short fibres of wool, for example, needed scribbling, carding, spinning the yarn and dressing. Each geographical area specialised in the manufacture of different types of cloth. Halifax made lightweight worsted, shalloons, calimancoes, camblets and tammies. The final dressing, raising and shearing the cloth before dyeing it was carried out by skilled croppers and dressers in Halifax, Wakefield and Leeds, of which John Wigney (1731–1793), William Wigney's father, was probably one, judging from his descriptions on his marriage and death certificates as a 'Skircoat comber'.

Because of their poverty and lack of formal education, the first Wigneys left little mark on society. Yet since everyone in those days was a churchgoer, their baptisms, marriages and deaths are commemorated in Church of England church records, even if, as seems likely, they were nonconformists. Documents such as maps, birth, marriage and death certificates, wills, newspaper advertisements and local histories, confirmed by a visit to the area in 2016, have enabled us to piece together the detailed history of the family, but only an outline is possible here.

During the eighteenth century it seems that the Wigneys were well established in Skircoat, a mile or two from the centre of Halifax, and that they were all involved in the clothing trade. Their fortunes were tied up with the well-established local families of Ramsden, Ryley, Bates, Pollitt and Wainhouse. The Wigneys occupied and owned part of smallholdings at Washer Lane[14] and Broad Gates,[15] now submerged in the richer suburbs of Halifax and Sowerby Bridge.[16] Wigney Ing,[17] a large meadow above Broad Gates, has also been built upon (see Figures 2.2, 2.3 and 2.4).

When the Hearth Tax[18] was collected in 1672, Soyland and Skircoat already stood out in the West Riding as the jewels in the crown, part of Daniel Defoe's 'noble scene of industry'. Whereas in many local villages more than half the houses only had a single hearth, in Skircoat 38 per cent had four hearths or more. A century later this area was the 'Silicon Valley' of Britain, where entrepreneurs funded imaginative new ideas for using the mechanisation of the cloth industry to make it even more cost-effective, and manufactured steam engines.

Figure 2.2: Old house at Washer Lane where William and Joseph Wigney grew up. Elizabethan in origin, it was occupied by the Waterhouse and Wainhouse families. There were several cottages and a mill nearby, some occupied by Wigneys in the eighteenth century. Drawing by Arthur Comfort. 'Sketches of Old Halifax', *Halifax Courier* (1911–12).

Figure 2.3: Broad Gates (Underbank), 1912. Many traces of a fifteenth-
century timber building, later encased in stone. Owned by Wainhouses
and Listers and by Thomas Wigney etc. to 1804, it was bought by son-
in-law Thomas Pollitt in 1806. There were several associated cottages
nearby. Wigney Ing was three fields upslope to the north.
Drawing by Arthur Comfort. 'Ancient Halls in and about Halifax',
Halifax Courier (1912–13).

Figure 2.4: Current view looking down Washer Lane from the top of
the Wainhouse Tower (1875), the tallest folly in Britain. The mill
complex is in the far distance but Wainhouse built the dye works (in
the middle distance) on the site of the Wigney cottages.

The main line represented by the Wigney surname begins with James (1707–1762) who married Alice Ryley (1711–1762) and had at least eight children, most of whom settled in the Huddersfield, Wakefield, Sowerby Bridge and Manchester areas. The Ryleys (Rileys)[19] were well established at Soyland, in Calderdale, three and a half miles from Halifax, not far from Skircoat and near Sowerby Bridge. For instance, as early as 1336 a messuage and 20 acres in Soyland were leased to Gilbert Ryley.[20] A Ryley had turned down a knighthood from Charles I in 1542. When the Hearth Tax was collected on Lady Day, 1642, ten houses in Soyland were occupied by Ryleys, and so on. The Ryleys had much more solid local foundations than the Wigneys.

James, supported by a large network of local Ryleys, may have even attained some importance.[21] The fact that the Wigneys sold property around Halifax from time to time suggests that they worked hard enough to own it, and these properties were sold in groups, because a commune of property owners in one place had combined forces to carry out the early aspects of cloth manufacture on one site. The next step up the social commercial ladder would be as a clothier, organising the whole production of cloth and taking it to Halifax market. Merchants, who made the real profits, dealt nationally at least, and most of the cloth ultimately found its way to London. Local drapers, though, sold cloth and clothes to the local gentry.

Life was tough. Most of James and Alice's children died very young. Among the exceptions was their eldest son John, the father figure of all the Brighton Wigneys. Like father, like son. Just as his father James had married into a well-off local family, John married Martha Bates. The Bates family were rife in the area, and still are. Once again, John may well have benefited from an established network of local contacts in organising a small group of hard-working cloth-makers with a range of skills, and distributing his manufactures. Towards the end of the eighteenth century, the traditional cloth trade in the area probably declined as further mechanisation continued and cloth manufacture became exploited by mill owners, who concentrated the various skills in one place and ultimately employed hundreds of workers. Indeed, Martha's relative, Timothy Bates may have contributed to this by establishing what began as Halifax's first cloth factory (Bates & Pollitt, Clothier) near Bank House in Sowerby Bridge in 1786. This soon became a foundry, one of the best-known manufacturers of steam engines in the world, with up to 500 workers.

John Wigney (1731–1793) and Martha Bates (b. 1734) probably lived at Washer Lane until 1775. At the start of their marriage (1751)[22] they probably lived much as Daniel Defoe had described – John is called a 'cloth dresser' in a court case in 1771,[23] and a 'comber' on his death certificate. They had ten children. Their sons, after being employed in cloth production from an early age, probably became engaged in taking cloth by packhorse to Halifax market and selling it there. John and Martha had four particularly significant sons. Their first, John II (b. 1754) stayed locally, became a cloth draper in Warley and produced the many descendants of note in Yorkshire mentioned in the next chapter.

William (1756–1836), the central figure in this book (Chapter 4) became a Brighton magnate. Joseph (1759–1795), something of a rolling stone, joined the army, died young but turned out to be the ancestor of most of the modern Wigneys in London, Oxford, Australia and the USA (see Chapter 6). Very much the youngest, Robert, 'Gypsy Bob' (1775–1834), never settled down and became a politically aware radical, first in London and then in Brighton, but first spent much of his life trading cloth from his packhorses (Chapter 5).

John's grandfather, Robert Wigney had married Judith Ramsden in 1704. Robert and Judith had two sons apart from James: Thomas (b. 1710) and George (b. 1712). George's son Thomas II (1736–1803)[24] became a successful property owner, ultimately owning Broad Gates, and one of his daughters, Sarah, married Thomas Pollitt, subsequently an industrialist. One of John's brothers, James II (1739–1813), a cloth dresser, also raised a family at Washer Lane and became successful, advertising for an apprentice in 1790. So there were several parallel Wigney families in the area, perhaps living in separate cottages on the same site.

We cannot account for some individuals. For example, a ne'er-do-well, James Wigney, was convicted for arrears in payments towards a bastard child in 1720 and 1725, when the child was being cared for by a Riley. James was fined a shilling in 1723 for an assault, and whipped and sent to Bradford House of Correction for another in 1728. In 1747 James Wigney/Wignall was deported for seven years for an assault, and for stealing a handkerchief, a goose and a shilling.

The relevant properties were all within a mile and a half of one another (see Figure 2.5). We imagine that for most of the seventeenth century the family occupied the cottages around the Old House at Denton Ings off Washer Lane. This house, beside the steep hill on the old road from Rochdale to Halifax, had been built around 1580. John must have been well off, because in 1775 (with Timothy Bates) he put the freehold of the fulling mill in Sowerby Bridge, established since about 1300, up for sale.[25]

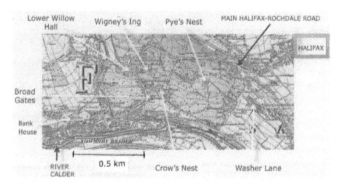

Figure 2.5: Map, based on First Edition of Ordnance Survey (1853), showing the area between Halifax and Sowerby Bridge, on the steep hillside overlooking the River Calder. It shows the main homesteads[26] occupied by the Wigneys and their associates. The parish of Skircoat is on the right-hand side; the parish of Warley is on the left.

John's brother James II advertised several cottages at Denton Ings for freehold sale in 1781. By then the four eldest of John's six sons, at least, had certainly left home. In the same year, the copyhold Broad Gates estate nearby was up for sale, probably including the three large fields above to the east of the Halifax–Rochdale turnpike road, which later came to be called Wigney Ing. The various Wigney families probably moved there in 1781. Thomas II put three closes to the north of the Broad Gates estate up for sale in 1784, James II took on an apprentice in 1790, Thomas II tried to sell Broad Gates in 1795 but died there and had written his will from Broad Gates in 1804. After John's death in 1793 Martha probably moved to a cottage in Shaw Hill[27] in Halifax (the current home of Halifax Town Football Club) but sold it in 1804, moving back to Broad Gates to help with the care of her grandchildren.

The move of restless young men away from Sowerby Bridge may have been due at least partly to the industrialisation of weaving. Sowerby Bridge led the way. Large fulling and raising mills were operating by 1758 and the first fully integrated woollen mill complex was established at Sowerby Bridge by 1778. Families who operated from home ultimately could not compete. At the same time, transport links with the outside world, such as the Aire and Calder navigation canal (1770), bringing coal, wool and food from the port at Hull, made the locals even more aware of opportunities elsewhere. Above all, contact with clothiers and merchants at market, and the plush lifestyles they enjoyed in the newly built Georgian houses at Skircoat, must have made the hard-working local lads envious.

No wonder that three of John Wigney and Martha Bates's sons, William, Joseph and Robert, moved away, where the commercial prospects were brighter. From their early teens, they probably helped their parents in combing and finishing, and later rode on horseback with cloth to Halifax or even Leeds markets, learning the value of money and to bargain and sell. Judging from their subsequent successes, they seem to have been well-educated and to have acquired a strong sense of social responsibility, perhaps derived in part from their strong nonconformist religious faith, basically Unitarian (Presbyterian) mixed with Quaker. It seems unlikely that they attended one of the local grammar schools, because these were only available to young men of high family and the well-to-do. Although there were at least four local grammar schools by the end of the seventeenth century, and Sowerby GS existed from 1711, mass education did not take off in the area until the 1820s.[28]

The Wigney surname in Yorkshire gradually petered out; the last we heard of was Iain Wigney, killed in a motor-bicycle accident in 2009. William moved out of Yorkshire for London, perhaps around 1775-1777 in his early twenties, to be followed later by his brothers Joseph and Robert ('Gypsy Bob').

In 1782, William married Ann Killick, from a family of Brighton fishing folk, at St Nicholas' Church in Brighton. Their first child was born in London, but then the Wigney focus moves further south, to Brighton, where William established himself. Eighteen years later, William, who by then had a young growing family, was joined by his nephew George Adolphus Wigney.

As we shall see, the futures of both their families were tied up with Brighton for many years. William left many descendants with considerable social status and financial assets. Their behaviour, however, was often wayward. Surprisingly, the bankruptcy of Wigney's Brighthelmston Bank in 1842 seems to have had little impact on their prospects. In contrast, the descendants of their cousin, George Adolphus Wigney, were upright characters, many with strong religious convictions, but considerably poorer. Their limited social status may have stemmed ultimately from William's disapproval of GA's marriage to the daughter of a 'tradesman'. So even if William had no money when he left Skircoat in about 1775 at the age of nineteen, he had skills and prospects.

3

THE ONES WHO STAYED BEHIND

B Y THE TIME the remaining Wigneys moved from Washer Lane to Broad Gates in about 1781, John's brother James II, a cloth dresser and his children were very much in evidence. So were John himself, his wife Martha (Bates), and John's nephew Thomas II (b. 1736), living at Broad Gates with his wife Lydia and four daughters.

Of John and Martha's children, we know that William (b. 1756, Chapter 4) was in London and Brighton by then and Joseph (b. 1759, Chapter 6) was in the army. All we can find about James III (b. 1762) was that he married Sally Barker and had four children. Thomas III (b. 1769) was only twelve years old in 1781. After marrying Rebecca Clark he probably moved away, because their first child Edward was born in 1798 in Doncaster. He ultimately became Edward of Hull, an auctioneer, and his son Edward William (b. 1831) emigrated to Canada in 1866 with Clara, establishing the vigorous Wigney population in Ottowa. John and Martha's youngest son, Robert, 'Gypsy Bob' (b. 1775, Chapter 5) was only six at the time of the probable move to Broad Gates.

John's eldest son, John Wigney II (b. 1754), is mentioned as a cloth draper in Warley in 1771.[1] This suggests that even at the age of seventeen, instead of being involved in the relentless daily grind of cloth production, he had begun to sell the cloth he had acquired in local markets. Perhaps this served as a role model for his brother William, two years younger, who ultimately became a Brighton draper for nearly twenty years (Chapter 4). John II married Tabitha Jennings in 1776.[2] She was also from Warley, the parish which occupies a narrow segment of land between Skircoat and Sowerby. They lived at Skircoat, most likely in one of the Broad Gates properties, and ultimately had six children.

Two of their daughters married Cronhelm brothers who, with the Cronhelms' father, had begun to work for the Edwards family at Pye's Nest nearby. This large estate, sloping to the west of Skircoat, was ultimately to become a major international industrialised clothing company, and was immediately north east of Broad Gates. The Cronhelms were refugees. Their father was Wilhelm George Otto von Cronhelm (1742–1813), originally a colonel in the King's Hanoverian Army. He dropped the 'von' when he was demobbed at Plymouth in 1782. With, his second wife and five youngest children he moved to Halifax in 1796 as language teacher and advisor to Sir Henry Edwards, JP, CB, Bart, the wealthy local landowner.

Elizabeth Wigney (1794–1846) married in 1811 his oldest son, Frederick William Cronhelm,[3] subsequently mill manager and accountant for Sir Henry. Nine years later, sister Alice Wigney[4] (b. 1790) married another son, G. Otto Cronhelm, a bookkeeper,[5] but he died two years afterwards, at the age of 27.

Elizabeth and Frederick brought up their six children in the Pye's Nest and later the Crow's Nest properties adjoining Broad Gates. F.W. Cronhelm was obviously very talented. He wrote some poetry and other works, edited the *Halifax Guardian* for three years, was the best chess player in Yorkshire, but above all, invented the system of double-entry bookkeeping which is still in use all over the world today. His 375-page book *Double*

Entry by Single: A New Method of Book Keeping was published in 1818. Other works included *The Rivers and Streams of Halifax* (1847) and *Thoughts on the Controversy as to the Plurality of Worlds* (1851). He was 'lucid in philosophical thought, and bright in glowing imagination'. At least, even after many of her Wigney relatives had moved away or died, Elizabeth kept the Wigney flag flying in the area. Once she had died, Frederick, at the age of 60, married a seventeen-year-old and had three more children.

Another of John Wigney II's children, William II (1784–1861) began as a farmer, but soon moved to Huddersfield, five miles away, to become a bank clerk. In 1809 he had married the daughter of a cloth dealer turned publican, Anne Townsend, whose father was the landlord of the (old) George Inn, Huddersfield's premier coaching inn for around 250 years.[6] When his bank failed, William became the landlord of the White Hart. Huddersfield was still a village at around that time, but expanded rapidly, quadrupling in population between 1800 and 1850 as numerous mills were established and Edgerton, the suburb which is the 'Belgravia of Huddersfield', began to be built. When Ann's father retired to farm at Netherton Moor two or three miles to the south, after running the George for eighteen years, William II took it over. So this was another case in which, by marrying into a well-established family, a Wigney male, probably unwittingly, gained access to social status and financial success.

William II, an ebullient and very sociable character, ran this very successful enterprise for 24 years (1816–1840).[7] So he was the publican of the George in the Market Place at the same time as his uncle William was in his prime as a Brighton banker. It proved to be the hub of the growing town, with activities including auctions, hustings, meetings, elections, subscription concerts and riots. 'The bar at the George was ... nightly thronged with the choice spirits of the town, who resorted there to learn and tell the news, to crack the joke ... and to imbibe the nut-brown ale, the choice wines, or the still more fiery waters of the house.'[8] William was self-important. When he detected misdemeanours he did not prosecute the miscreant, but asked them to make a public confession in the *Leeds Mercury* instead, for example

> I, Bessy Mitchell, chambermaid at the George Inn, Huddersfield, did receive in an improper manner, from a lady who slept at the above inn, and left early that morning, the sum of three shillings beside one shilling the lady gave me as chambermaid, for the use of the bed, knowing that such a charge was contrary to the usage of the house, where the most upright conduct is shown ... on my acknowledging my crime, and publishing this advertisement, Mr Wigney has kindly stopped proceedings, for which I thank him... (24 December 1817).

When William II eventually retired to farm at Netherton Moor, and sought a new tenant to manage the hotel, the advertisement suggested that the tenancy included two nearby dwelling houses, an extensive range of stabling and coach houses, warehouses, shops let to woollen and cloth merchants, and other conveniences, together with about 40 acres of land. Much of this was copyhold, because it was owned by the influential Ramsden family. William had accumulated a large collection of sophisticated oil paintings and watercolour drawings, which he returned to Huddersfield annually to exhibit on a large scale.[9] Apart from farming, he acted as an overseer of the poor, and a surveyor of highways.

In fact one of his sons, Thomas Jennings Wigney, who was in private practice as a surgeon in Huddersfield after having been a house surgeon at the Huddersfield and

Upper Agbrigg Infirmary, then took on the tenancy of the George for 26 years, from 1840 onwards.

Figure 3.1: The George Hotel, Huddersfield (2016).

We do not know why he changed profession, but his wife was the daughter of an innkeeper. He supervised the move of the George to new premises, at first owned by the Ramsden family, from its dominant position in Huddersfield's Market Square to a site next to the new railway station. The result was an impressive Grade II listed building, designed by the architect William Wallen, which graces the square. The railway station, with the most elegant railway façade in Britain, had been built nearby a few years earlier on land leased from Thomas. Until recently, The George Inn has been Huddersfield's premier watering hole.[10] It bears a blue plaque commemorating the foundation there in 1895 of Rugby League football, and there is a commemorative display inside.

But, by the time Thomas Jennings had also retired to farm at Netherton, like his father and grandfather before him, the hotel business was never as lucrative again. Two of William's sons became well-known, though, as Wigney portrait photographers in the late 1850s and 1860s. They established their businesses in Huddersfield and Scarborough, which at that time was an elegant spa town. They were in at the start of commercial photography and one of them, J.T. Wigney, has seven photographs in the National Portrait Gallery.

Wigneys persisted in the Huddersfield area for some time. We are frequently offered, on eBay, stone porter jars from the Wigney Brewery, Huddersfield, dated 1860–1910 produced by a Wigney brewery and Thomas J Wigney & Son, Importers of Wines and Spirits, 33 & 35 John William Street, Huddersfield.

Eventually, though, the other three sons of John Wigney from Skircoat, William, Robert and Joseph, made more of a splash by moving away from Yorkshire. We tell the tales of their lives in the next few chapters.

PART II

BRIGHTON –
BOOM & BUST

4

WILLIAM WIGNEY
& GEORGIAN BRIGHTON

W HAT MAKES a successful businessman? Allied
to the ability to work hard and considerable
flexibility, there must be an element of luck,
of being in the right place at the right time. William
Wigney not only found himself in Regency Brighton at
the peak of its popularity, but had the good fortune to
marry into a Brighton family with established business
interests, and to live there in Brighton's heyday for
another fifty years.

Brighton's eventual success

Brighthelmston originated as a poor fishing village only
fifty miles from London, between Shoreham, the centre of
the shipbuilding industry, and Newhaven. Hove hardly
existed until the 1820s (see Figure 4.5, p. 64). Lewes, the
administrative capital of Sussex, was eight miles away,
laced with impressive mansions and country gentlemen. In
1750 Brighthelms-ton's population of about two thousand
was dominated by fisherfolk, some of whom lived in
shacks on the shingly beach. They put to sea in small boats
and laid out their nets to dry on the Staithe, an open area to
the east with a stream flowing to the sea. By 1850 its

situation had hardly altered since Daniel Defoe dropped by in about 1715:

> The sea is very unkind to this town, and has by its continual encroachments, so gained upon them, that in a little time more they might reasonably expect it would eat up the whole town, above 100 houses having been devoured by the water in a few years past; they are now obliged to ... beg money all over England, to raise banks against the water; the expense of which ... will be eight hundred pounds; which if one were to look at the town, would seem to be more than all the houses ... are worth.[1]

It was not until 1821 that an effective sea defence began to be constructed.

The commercial development of Brighton really began because of the popularity of sea bathing. Dr Richard Russell and others wrote books in the 1750s extolling the virtues of total immersion in salt water as cures for all manner of common ailments. Wooden, horse-drawn, wheeled bathing machines had appeared on the shingle, manned by brawny women mainly from fisherfolk families. Once these machines, with suitably clad paying guests on board, had been dragged into the waves, avoiding the polluted shore, the bathers were submerged time and time again in the water. The sea bathing at Brighton was even mentioned by Jane Austen in *Pride and Prejudice*.

Brighton was at its lowest ebb in 1761, when there were 400 families, only a quarter of whom were well off enough to pay rates, with 35 people in the poor house. By 1794 there were 5,700 residents and 10,000 visitors a year, and by 1817–19, 18,000 residents and 19,700 annual visitors. The town was called 'Piccadilly by the seaside' by William Wilberforce.[2] Then, Brighthelmston had room to expand further, first towards the South Downs to the north, and then sideways, by the construction of Brunswick Terrace and Kemp Town 'which were attached like a pair of wings to either end of the Georgian Town in the early 1820s'.[3]

Originally, in the 1760s, there were only six main streets; the boundaries of the village were set by East Street, North Street parallel to the beach, and West Street, with St Nicholas's Church on a hillock to the north. Middle Street and Ship Street ran down from North Street towards the sea. There were two small lodging houses, the Castle Hotel near the Staithe and the Ship Inn (Figure 4.1).

Dr Russell built himself an impressive house beside the shingle at the edges of the Staithe, the house which, after his death, was occupied by the Duke of Cumberland, the Prince Regent's uncle, who began to visit Brighton regularly in 1771. The Duke of Marlborough also bought a house there. The next ten years were vibrant, as well-off visitors from London established a flourishing society. Six schools for young gentlemen and boarding schools for young ladies appeared, together with drapers, milliners and vintners.

Figure 4.1: Brighton in 1788 (Budgen's Map). By that time it had become an important resort for London society, with frequent coaches to and from London and Lewes. There were only six main streets and the building of the Pavilion had not yet begun.

Even by 1766, Brighton, only 57 miles from London, had 'become one of the principal places in the Kingdom for the resort of the idle and dissipated as well as the diseased and the infirm'.[4] Compared to the other resorts popular with the upper classes, such as Scarborough, Margate, Bath, Epsom, Tunbridge Wells, Cheltenham, Harrogate and Malvern, Brighton was the earliest to have the full range of facilities. Most were in place by 1773. It had bathing machines (1754), seawater baths (1769), a spa (1760), coffee houses (1752), libraries (1759), a theatre troupe for the season (1764), a theatre (1774), an MC and organised social life, such as balls (mid-1760s), gardens and promenades such as the Steine (1750), lodging houses (1750), hunts (1750s), races (1783), public breakfasts (1771) and a 'Season' (1779). Improvement commissioners (established 1773) ensured that the activities of the fishermen were gradually phased out, sewerage and street lighting were modernised and ultimately that a proper road along the seafront was constructed (1821).

All these rich visitors spent so much money that Brighton was in a 'bubble'. Brighton sucked in all sorts of trades and professions, purveyors of luxury goods and services, such as linen drapers (as William Wigney was originally),[5] doctors, surgeons, apothecaries, jewellers, silversmiths, dressmakers, milliners, shoemakers, furniture makers, carpenters, artists, butchers, bakers, cooks, confectioners, private tutors, brewers and publicans, It was relatively unaffected by the French Revolutionary Wars (1793–1802) and Napoleonic Wars (1803–15) with France.[6] Indeed, the influx of soldiers from temporary tents and barracks, their hangers-on and their horses, stimulated the local economy. This was at a time when harsh and unpopular national taxes were imposed to pay for the conflicts, the volatile economy caused numerous failures of local banks, and the Enclosure Acts caused much agricultural poverty. Brighton seems to have been immune from these stresses of war.

So it was entirely natural that, like so many of those with whom he came into contact in Georgian London, William's attention should turn towards Brighton as a place which presented trading opportunities. In contrast to London, smelly, smoky and polluted, Brighton seemed, literally, a breath of fresh air. Some of William's contacts visited Brighthelmstone, as it was then called, to participate in the sea cures promoted by Dr Russell, and in any case, because there might be opportunities for smuggling with France on the schooners.

William Wigney becomes established in Brighton

William was solid, sensible and dependable, with an entrepreneurial streak, and it was natural that he should begin to make a living as a traveller selling the fine cloth made by his family and their associates in Yorkshire. He probably began to help on the family smallholding and in cloth production before his teens. We know that he was still in his father's house at Skircoat near Halifax in 1771, because, aged 15, he is mentioned in a court case as being next to John Wigney's house. His father was acquitted of slandering a woman neighbour, whilst his four sons looked on.

Between then and his marriage to Ann Killick in St Nicholas's Church in Brighton in 1782,[7] when he was aged 26, the factual trail goes cold. Our efforts to find out more about this period are mentioned in the next chapter. Nevertheless, on the basis of the contemporary scene and comments from Brighton writers and family authors, we can piece together a convincing story.

In William's day the major transport method for wool, cloth and other goods were the packhorse routes. Individual horses, horses chained together, or donkeys, could travel 15 miles a day over hills in West Yorkshire, 25 miles a day on the flat, with each horse carrying well-balanced loads of 150–250 lbs.[8] The packhorse men stayed overnight en route at packhorse inns. Numerous routes criss-crossed the Pennines and West Yorkshire. From London to Brighton there were three well-used routes. The main one to Brighton, turnpiked in 1770 for carriages, went close to the George at Crawley, near to what is now Gatwick Airport. Another went east before turning south to Lewes. The third followed the Roman Stane Way via Chichester. Since there is no major river or canal running from London to Brighton it was not until 1841, when the railway came to Brighton, that pack-horses were superseded.

William probably graduated from taking cloth to market to being a London cloth trader. By the late 1770s, he was possibly living with relatives in London and trading this cloth and lace with London shops. These shops provided curtains and dresses for the emerging middle classes who were moving into the new houses being built in the Georgian terraces in central London. He may have brought some of the cloth himself by packhorse from his home or from Leeds market. Although an increasing proportion of this cloth from the north probably arrived at London with coal shipped from the Yorkshire coalfields, the network of packhorse routes extended to Brighton. William's younger brother Robert, 'Gypsy Bob' (see Chapter 5), probably led this a nomadic existence as such an itinerant dealer from 1804 until about 1825.

We know that William had links with central London because he was living in Great St Thomas the Apostle

Street on his marriage (23 April 1782) and his first child, was christened at 'Fleet Street, St. Bride's' in 1783, when William was living in the City of London.[9] He could well have traded between London and the provinces. Perhaps he even visited Brighton, and crossed the Channel on one of the regular schooner services between Brighton or Newhaven, and Dieppe. Otherwise, it is a mystery where he first met his wife, Ann Killick, from a well-established family of Brighton fisherfolk.

Ann's father, Robert, had been the captain of the *Princess Caroline,* plying the route between Newhaven and Dieppe at least until 1776. Then he traded in wine and coal in Brighton. Perhaps William and Ann met on one of William's trading trips from Brighton to France or in Brighton. Another possibility is that Ann was staying with a relative, John Killick (1713–1784) at Whitehall, Cheam, near Ewell, where there is still a well-known packhorse bridge, when she met William.

Establishing themselves in Brighton from 1783 or 1784 onwards, William lived to 80 and Ann to 99, a considerable age for those times. They founded the Wigney dynasty there, based on the drapery store William began in North Street. They were helped by the inheritance they received when Ann's father died in 1796, and by William's considerable business experience and acumen.

When they married, William was 26 and Anne was 22. Perhaps Ann was by then in service in London, but that seems unlikely because her father was soon classed as a 'gentleman' in the first Brighton directories.

Imagine that William arrived in London in about 1776 at the age of twenty, and was based there for seven years. Where did he live and what contacts did he make? At that time the Newington Green Unitarian Chapel was particularly active, and included individual Quakers such as William Blake (in London 1776–83), whose father was a haberdasher, and Clio Rickman, who had published some of Thomas Paine's poetry and was later to publish Paine's *The Rights of Man*. This was published in 1791 on Paine's return from America and after the French Revolution. This book had a massive international influence.

Clio Rickman came from Lewes, the county town of Sussex, seven miles from Brighton, where his father, a Quaker, kept the Bear Inn. As a teenager, he had met Thomas Paine during Paine's spell as an Excise Officer in Lewes from 1768 to 1774, which ended when he himself was allegedly involved in smuggling. During his time in Lewes, Paine visited Brighton to attend the chapel established by the devout Lady Huntingdon, who knew both American presidents George Washington and Thomas Jefferson. It is possible that Paine had met both Washington and Jefferson in London at Newington Green Unitarian Chapel. After responding to a letter of introduction to someone in Pennsylvania from Benjamin Franklin, Paine went to America, supporting the American War of Independence, Washington, Franklin and the abolition of slavery.

Clio Rickman's brother, Thomas Rickman, was a partner in a Brighton bank which failed in 1793. He subsequently established the Brighthelmstone Bank in partnership with William Wigney from 1797 onwards.[10] William Blake himself rented a cottage at Felpham,[11] on the Brighton side of Bognor, from 1800 to 1803, where he wrote *Jerusalem*. Both Blake and Clio Rickman are buried at Bunhill Fields, in north London, where Quakers were buried en masse in unmarked graves. So it is possible that during his time in London, William Wigney established a network of nonconformist contacts which stood him in good stead.

According to George Adolphus's son Frederick, by then a successful newspaper editor in Australia, writing in *Past and Present*, William arrived in Brighton with a donkey loaded with drapery, and became involved in smuggling and selling coal.[12] There is probably a grain of truth in this story, written more than eighty years after the event. In *Glimpses of Our Ancestors in Sussex* (1885), Charles Fleet, the well-informed ex-editor of the *Sussex Advertiser*, suggests that smuggling might have attracted William to Brighthelmston. Earlier, in the *History of Brighthelmstone* (1862), John Ackeron Erredge had gone further:

> Captain Killick's daughter was married to Mr William Wigney, a north countryman, who had then recently settled in Brighton, in North Street, where he kept a linen-drapers shop. The house … which he paid for in French money, which he had received in exchange for English coin from the refugees brought over by his father-in-law. It is related of him that he was not over-scrupulous in the way of business, of passing half-franc pieces for six pences to the unwary. He was afterwards the head of the firm of Messrs Wigney, Rickman & Co, Bankers, Steine Lane.

This book, however, is riddled with so many factual errors that we might give William the benefit of the doubt. Perhaps some resented his success.

Indeed, smuggling seems to have been an established Brighton practice. In the local newspapers, there are many references to smugglers, the seizure of contraband and skirmishes with French boats. Two inns mention that they were connected to the seafront, where contraband could be unloaded, by a network of underground tunnels. Coal could be unloaded at night to escape the local Coal Tax, imposed in 1777 to help to pay for improvements to the sea frontage. The Brighton–Dieppe ferry was ideal for smuggling, and the presence of the Royal Court in

Brighton created a demand for luxuries, such as French lace, which was met in this manner.

For example, when one French gentleman landed, lace was discovered beneath some fruit. In 1816, a young man was arrested for trying to smuggle cotton stockings and thread in stone bottles filled with spirits with false bottoms. Earlier, after the French Revolution some aristocrats were smuggled across to escape persecution, like the 21-year-old, pregnant, Comtesse de Noailles, who was met by the Prince Regent's mistress, Maria Fitzherbert. Presumably such aristocrats brought some of their francs with them, to be converted into British coinage by William Wigney's bank.

Prominent amongst the fisherfolk families were the numerous Killicks, the earliest of whom we encounter in 1548. One of the Killick family was Martha Gunn, the most famous of those women who operated the bathing machines. She was still dipping the Prince Regent at the age of 84. Robert and Cornelius Killick had been sea captains operating schooners which plied weekly between Newhaven and Dieppe. After abandoning the *Princess Caroline* in 1776, Robert operated a brewery, acted as a wine merchant and traded coal in Ship Street. He was living at 24 West Street, a prestigious address, when he died in 1796.

William and Ann quickly started a family: Grace, born in London, appeared in 1782; Robert, who died in infancy, in 1783; and Mary Anne in 1784. It was in about 1783 that William and Ann moved to Brighton, the same year that the Prince of Wales, son of George III, later the Prince Regent (1811) paid his first visit at the age of 21. It seems likely that at first, they lived with Ann's father in Ship Street or 24 West Street. William and Ann brought up eleven children in Brighton, and despite their working-class backgrounds, they and their descendants became rich pillars of the local political and commercial scene. When William died in 1836, his Estate was worth over £20 million in today's terms. Ann lasted to the age of 99 in 1859.

How did William manage to accumulate such wealth? He was a young businessman with financial and entrepreneurial experience and links with the cloth trade in London and Leeds. He was a nonconformist. Brighton's nonconformists were well-established and deeply embedded in the local business community and amongst the 'Commissioners'. A nonconformist school had been established in 1660, the Unitarian (Presbyterian) chapel in Union Street was built in 1683 and the Quakers had had a chapel and burial ground since 1701. William had strong trading links, legal and illegal, through the Killicks' ferries across the Channel and the importation of coal by sea. Brighton and its visitors expanded rapidly.

Ann's father left Ann and William a substantial legacy in 1796 which enabled William to diversify into brewing, public houses and coal. Soon afterwards, he ventured into banking; like many local banks established at the time, a natural development for a successful merchant. His bank in Steine Lane was in an ideal position, near the commercial centre of the town, very close to the arrival and departure area for stagecoaches in Castle Square, and close to the Prince Regent's home.

Soon after his arrival in Brighthelmston William set up a draper's shop in North Street, dealing in fine cloth and clothes. In his drapery store, he began to deal in credit, and establish a reputation for financial probity. So it was natural for him to take over the local Lewes bank owned by Richard Peters and Rickman which failed in 1794. The declaration of war against the French in 1793 created financial instability – banks and businesses crashed – in the first eight months of 1793 alone there were 873 commissions for bankruptcies amongst merchants nationwide. William, though, turned the bank, with Thomas Rickman, into more or less his own bank, the Brighthelmston Bank, in 1797. Local trade received a massive boost from 1793 onwards, when an army camp was established nearby, at least in the summer months, on the current site of Regency Square westwards, to counteract the threat of French invasion. By 1795, up to 10,000 troops trebled Brighton's population at a stroke.[13] Apart from the burgeoning sales of clothes and beer, the army rented William's extensive Wigney stables off Spring Walk in 1801 to accommodate a hundred cavalry.[14]

William and Ann's young family was augmented unexpectedly in 1795. William's younger brother Joseph had led a much less fortunate life. Born in 1759, he was married, like William, in 1782 and then lived in Manchester, where his first three children were born. Once he had left military service, he tried his luck as a trader in London but bankruptcy ensued in 1792 and he returned to the army. He died in Ireland in August 1795, as a quartermaster in the cavalry, as a result of being kicked on the head by a horse. His widow, Elizabeth, died later that year, it is said, 'of a broken heart', leaving three children, two of whom William took under his wing in Brighton. George Adolphus was five and Frederick Charles was two. At the time, in his Brighton house, William had four children at home, son Henry had recently died of infectious disease and wife Ann was pregnant with Isaac Newton. William and Ann just about coped with the extra domestic responsibility, but perhaps George Adolphus and Frederick Charles never quite fitted in (see Chapters 6 and 7).

When his father-in-law Robert Killick, the ex-sea captain, died in 1796, leaving £5,000, William and Ann seem to have received a substantial sum. This may have allowed William to exploit new opportunities. Killick had four daughters, one of whom had died, and one surviving son. Ann had married William Wigney, Maria was married to Philip Vallance, a brewer, wine and coal merchant, and Kitty's husband was John Turner. Killick left £1,700 to Ann and Kitty and £700 to be divided between his sons in law William Wigney and John Turner. In addition,

> I give to William Wigney my copyhold messuage or tenement coach house buildings, grounds, hereditaments and premises being in West Street, Brighthelmston – permit my wife Ann Killick full use, occupation and enjoyment – rents etc. – afterwards permit Sarah Killick [unmarried daughter] to do the same – then when she dies, auction the premises and give money to Sarah's children –or if she has none, divide between Ann and Kitty.[15]

So in effect, William inherited his brewery and coal merchant franchise at 24 West Street.[16] Once again, with a vengeance, a Wigney proved to have married into a well-established and fairly well-off local family, just as his father and grandfather had done, this time in a rapidly expanding town with excellent economic prospects.

He began to invest in the burgeoning number of public houses. Ultimately, in 1802, he abandoned the drapery, which in 1808 became Hannington & Sons,[17] the famous store which existed into the 1970s, making Brighton 'the marine West End of London'. By 1802, of course, apart from his involvement in the bank, he already owned several public houses, a brewery and a coal merchant.

The pressures on Brighton required more sophisticated governance. The equivalent of a Town Council, of up to 64 elders known as 'Commissioners', had been created in 1773 to administer roads, lighting, sewerage, law and order and town expansion. William became involved by

1794, when he was elected High Constable for the first time. For example, in 1804, when the Prince Regent petitioned to create New Road, moving a road westwards to allow him to expand the new Brighton Pavilion without interference, William seconded the motion when it was put to the Commissioners. At one time or another his sons George, Isaac Newton and Clement were all Commissioners, and had an important influence on the town's development.

In the first years of the nineteenth century, when the expansion of Brighton was at its zenith. William moved up the social scale. It is interesting that Wigney enterprises are not mentioned in Cobby's Brighthelmston Trades Directory of 1800; perhaps by then he considered 'trade' beneath him. James, John and Thomas did not appear amongst his sons' names; Isaac Newton, Clement, Henry and George were new Wigney family names, and so were Grace, Harriet and Charlotte. His bank, situated in a prime position, served many of the aristocracy, whilst his brewery, numerous public houses and judicial purchases of new letting houses for not only made him rich, but placed him at the hub of local social life. New churches, Evangelical, Presbyterian and Catholic, sprang up and William and his young family began to worship at the Union Chapel in Upper Ship Street, near his home, rather than at St Nicholas's Church, which was high church and dominated by the highly conservative, rich and influential Wagner family. William sold his family pew there in 1801.[18]

Alongside the improvement in his social status, we can speculate that William's accent gradually lost its northern lilt and became more upper-crust, either by design or by unconscious assimilation of the vowels and diphthongs of those with whom he was in day-to-day contact.

Figure 4.2 William's children appear to have had a sophisticated education. This is an original graphite drawing of Raglan Castle by Clement Wigney (circa 1820).

As the London aristocracy disembarked from their stagecoaches outside his bank, or trawled his drapers shop nearby for appropriately stunning formal clothes, his accent, dress and mannerisms probably altered appropriately.

So, by 1810, William, at 54 was very well established in Brighton as a well-respected banker, brewer and Commissioner. His surviving children had been privately educated in Brighton. Grace (28) had already married Joseph Lee, Martha (26) had married Trayton Pagden, a wine and spirit merchant, soon to have eight children. William III the younger was 23 and George was 21. Harriet (20) was at home for another ten years. Isaac Newton was 15, Clement was 10 and Charlotte was 8. William was still in touch with his nephews, George Adolphus (GA, 20) and Frederick Charles (17). By that time GA had returned to the Brighton/Chichester area after a spell in the militia (Norfolk Regiment, see Chapter 6), and Frederick Charles was already in India, embarking on an army career (Chapter 7).[19]

Although his son William III had married Sarah Podmore by 1815 and left home, we can speculate that William's premises in Brighton, as the growing town was called by then, had become crowded. William and Ann were rich enough to employ a cook and several servants but still had five maturing children at home. Where could William and Ann entertain their friends and acquaintances? Isaac Newton and George were moving in social circles where they would soon ride to hounds. If their parents moved out, their house in Brighton would allow the youngsters to flourish there instead. Brighton itself had become a noisy polluted place, full of building labourers, servants and prostitutes as well as the upper crust of Regency life – and diseases were rife. So from 1815 to 1826, William and Ann, joined at first by some of the children, rented Newtimber House, near Hassocks, from an acquaintance (see Preface).

This was seven miles from Brighton along country tracks, but although William was 59 years old in 1815 he commuted into Brighton in his horse-drawn carriage, and back again, every day. He continued as a Brighton Commissioner and to run the Brighthelmstone Bank. Even in 1825, during the monetary crisis which led to the demise of three other Brighton banks, a local records that William, 'old Mr Wigney', was still at his bank daily, reliably dispensing bank notes and credit.

> While older and older establishments in the town went down, when all credit seemed to have perished ... the stern-looking handsome old man took to his station each day at his counter, from the opening to the closing hour, with heavy bags of gold at his elbow, ready to pay in cash all demands.... Wigneys was soon voted 'As safe as the Bank of England' and the bank came out of the ordeal stronger than ever.[20]

By the time old William and Ann moved back into Brighton from Newtimber in 1826, their children were all off their hands or establishing careers of their own. Even his youngest child, Charlotte had been married at Newtimber to the Reverend Henry Butterfield. His sons Clement and Isaac Newton were gradually taking over the reins of the family bank in Brighton, with Isaac as the senior partner. Rickman had opted out in 1810. By 1826, Clement was married to Harriet Cowley and Isaac Newton had married Caroline Walter, the granddaughter of John Walter, the founder of *The Times* newspaper. William III had tried to establish a brewery in Kemp Town in 1824 with one of the founders of Kemp Town, Thomas Reade Kemp. Banker William's nephew George Adolphus, idiosyncratic and original, had started out on his own in brewing; indeed, he had already published a famous book about the scientific principles of brewing. Years earlier though, as we shall see later, he had become alienated from William the banker and the rest of his family.

George the brewer

George, William's son, had become the most successful. In his *Glimpses*, Charles Fleet calls him 'a solid, steady-going man, who kept to his beer-making and beer-selling'.[21] Firstly, he took over from William the Wigney and Co. family brewery and coalyard in Ship Street. Then he bought the house next door to live in. He married Sarah Russell and in 1818, they had a son, Frederick, destined to die in his teens in 1835.

Figure 4.3: The Beeches at Barcombe, where George the brewer lived c. 1826–42.

Promoted by his father, George also became a Town Commissioner, serving as High Constable of Brighton by 1822, and later as Treasurer of the Commissioners for ten years. One can imagine that he and his father together had considerable local influence and connections. By 1826, he was rich enough to rent The Beeches, a large house at Barcombe near Lewes, from Gabriel Egles (Figure 4.3).[22] There, he employed seven servants and a gardener. Sadly, Sarah died the following year, and is commemorated by a plaque in Barcombe Church.

Before long George married Elizabeth Podmore, sister of the wife of his brother, William III. They had ten children. George owned the lease of The Beeches until 1842, when he and Elizabeth moved back to Brighton. George continued to organise the successful Brighton brewery and its associated public houses for the rest of his life, and to be involved in civic affairs. Until 1842, he was also in partnership with his brother-in-law, Trayton Pagden, as Furner, Pagden & Wigney, wine and spirit merchants, of 17 Water Lane, Great Tower Street, London.

Before we explain what happened to William and Ann after they returned to Brighton from Newtimber House in 1826, let us first pursue the fates of these children, born to the brewers William III and George, and the two Podmore sisters to whom they were married.

William III's first-born, William (b. 1814) had a 'diseased brain' and died at 37. His other son, Robert II (b. 1816) married a Scot, Mary Band. They had two children, the younger of whom, William (b. 1845) was an Edinburgh accountant, considered very competent but lacking social skills.

Apart from Arthur and Albert, George's children were not particularly striking. Four died in infancy, whilst Clara (b. 1826) and Ellen (b. 1828) went to live with their aunt Martha Pagden at her husband Trayton's brewery at Church Street, Epsom. Clara married late but Ellen never married. Edgar (1834–1865) emigrated to New Zealand. Arthur and Albert went to sea. Captain Arthur Wigney (b. 1832), unmarried, was a 'daring and intrepid' seaman, once captain of the *Windsor Castle*, who died of a heart attack in 1872 when his ship, the *Cerberus* 'the prototype of all modern battleships'[23] was moored in Hobson's Bay near Melbourne. Albert (1842–1928) also turned out to be a courageous sea captain.

George's other son, George II, though, was not such a pillar of society. He moved to London in his early twenties and was discharged from the Christ Church workhouse in Southwark in March 1840. In the 1841 census he is recorded as a wine merchant living in London within the Walls (St Swithun, London Stone) and later as lodging in the Tower Ward of London near where one of his father's wine businesses was located. In 1845 he was found drunk and disorderly at Gravesend.

> George Wigney, a fashionably-attired young man, owner of the Jackall schooner ... was brought up in the custody of the police, charged with the following outrageous conduct... He would wander about the principal streets in the dead of the night, conducting himself in a very boisterous style, and was in the habit of dressing in the attire of something like Will Watch, the bold smuggler, with a pair of formidable pistols by his side, threatening serious mischief to anyone who dared to oppose his progress ... on Thursday night, when entering a thoroughfare not much known for its respectability, he was seen to pick up a stone and shy it through a window, completely demolishing it.[24]

When the police took him into custody, he vowed that he would shoot them all, and then declared that his hangers-on were brave fellows, all six feet and a half high, who would see justice done him. At the hearing, apparently repentant, George offered £5 to any charity the magistrate pleases, but was fined 40 shillings. When he could find neither, he was remanded to prison. George died at 32 in 1848 and perhaps was an alcoholic.

William's final years

After William and Ann moved back into Brighton, into a newly built house, William continued to be involved in local affairs, and of course, he still received the profits from his bank, the brewery, his public houses and his lettings. For years the bank had been issuing its own £5 and £10 bank notes, proudly signed by William (Figure 4.4), and thousands of these must have been in circulation in Brighton.[25] Now aged 70, William relinquished day-to-day control of the bank to his sons Isaac Newton and Clement – so much so that he may not have fully appreciated the various uses to which the bank's profits were being put.

Figure 4.4: Brighthelmston bank note, signed by William Wigney.

William's continuing activity in local affairs is confirmed by his presence at an important meeting at the Iron Duke in Waterloo Street in 1829. This public house now has an underground tunnel to the church over the road, enabling the clerics to nip under for a surreptitious drink. A plaque on the pub wall says it all:

Figure 4.5: The plaque in Waterloo Street, Brighton, commemorating the Foundation of Hove.[26]

The fields to the west of Brighton soon became a new suburb. The grand regency terraces which now dominate Hove were erected remarkably quickly. William and Ann moved into Brunswick Square as soon as their elegant house was completed.[27] He and Ann must have been very proud when their son Isaac Newton Wigney, married in 1822 Caroline Walter, the niece of John Walter, the editor of *The Times* throughout the French Wars. They must have been delighted when Isaac Newton was subsequently elected the first Whig MP for Brighton in 1832.

William died in 1836, at the age of 81, at his house in Brunswick Square. He left around 40 grandchildren. His meticulous 36-page will[28] mentions his assets, but of course does not take account of the considerable goodwill involved in the brewery and the bank. He acknowledges the value of the legacy provided by his wife's father Robert Killick, nearly 40 years earlier. He mentions the premises belonging to his sons William III and George by virtue of agreements in 1828 and 1833. He had sensibly begun to dispose of his assets before he died.

William left his share of the freehold of the core brewery premises in Ship Street to his four sons, and asks that they should pay into his estate the value, by arbitration, of his half share of the brewery business.

The bank premises and the business he leaves to Isaac Newton, George obtains all the premises on the east side of Middle Street, William III receives seven public houses, and Clement gains eleven, including the Regent Hotel (subsequently purchased by George Adolphus) plus six acres in Hurstmoncioux (Herstmonceux). Wife Ann gains a substantial annuity of £1,200 a year, plus his carriage and horses, and each of his daughters receives £800 plus property or other equivalent assets. Grace Amelia, for example, is given 18 Cannon Place and outbuildings, a coalyard and building in Ship Street, and shares in New Shoreham harbour, turnpike roads and the Globe Insurance Company.

William played a major role in the development of Brighton, and earned the respect of thousands, from all walks of life, who had dealt with him. As the *Bury & Norwich Post* put it (16 November 1836), it 'was a remarkable instance of what may be obtained by perseverance and integrity. Although he entered the town a stranger, he amassed a fortune reported to be £300,000.' Ann went to live with the Butterfields and then the Robinsons, until she died months short of her 100th birthday.[29]

William must have felt that he had left his bank in the remarkably safe hands of two of his sons, Isaac Newton – after all, he was an MP – and Clement. He had already discussed with Isaac Newton the investment of some money from the bank in a potentially lucrative venture to produce shawls from Merino wool in Glasgow.

His nephew George Adolphus Wigney, the brewer, and his best known son, Isaac Newton Wigney, the MP, had fascinating lives and descendants. We shall ultimately cover their life histories in detail, but the story now turns to Robert, William's youngest brother, the enigmatic 'Gypsy Bob'.

5

THE ENIGMA OF 'GYPSY BOB'

ROBERT WIGNEY, 'Gypsy Bob', William's youngest brother, was born in 1775.[1] So he was nineteen years younger than William, but from the same nonconformist and weaving roots. Presumably he was known as 'Gypsy' Bob because of his peripatetic life style. Certainly the nephew of his friends Daniel and William Constable, Clair James Grece, wrote in his journal that a friend had described Robert as an Egyptian, as he showed no signs of settling down.[2]

Our first evidence of Robert in Brighton was in 1798. No doubt he was attracted from the Halifax area to Brighton because he was invited by William, his successful older brother. Much of his life – say, between 1805 and 1824 – was probably spent as a travelling salesman of textiles, on the road between Leeds and London, and between London and Brighton. Then he lived in Brighton until he died there in 1834, at the age of 59.

Gypsy Bob never married, although a snippet from Daniel Constable's diary[3] (17 December 1798) suggests that he had some acquaintance with the opposite sex: 'walked to Croydon, some tender business for my friend Wigney with Miss R, saw the maid servant, got all the information I could and wrote to Wigney'. Robert did not settle down until he became a lodging-house keeper in Richmond Road, Brighton (now demolished) for the last nine years of his life.

Yet he did not merely keep all the segments of the far-flung Wigney family in touch with one another. He was a well-known character in his own right, a Quaker and a political radical, perhaps the most left wing of the Wigney clan. We know much about his life in his late teens and twenties, and in the years before his death at the age of 59, but little in between.

He is likely to have started trading from the Leeds markets south to London in about 1795, and he first visited Brighton 'on the road' in 1800. In 1799 Mr Whichelo sold The White Lion public house to William Wigney.

> This was the first house in Brighton that his brother, Mr Robert Wigney, put up at when he first came to Brighton as a travelling 'pack-man' – the house being at that time frequented by that class of 'commercials'.[4]

We have an insight into his life in London through the diaries of Daniel Constable of Horley Mill, Surrey. Horley Mill used to be a water and malt mill, with an adjacent shop which sold cloth and employed a tailor and seamstress. After a few years in London, Daniel worked for Daniel Hack, the kingpin of the Quakers in Brighton and a draper in North Street, before taking over, with his brother William Constable, William Wigney's drapery store in North Street from 1802 to 1806. He made a considerable success of this enterprise before the brothers travelled to North America, to explore the country as well as finding somewhere suitable for their family to live should they all emigrate.

After a brief interregnum, the Constables' shop became Hanningtons, the Harrods of Brighton, 'the marine West End of London', for over 150 years.[5] One of the aunts of Mary (Wilmshurst), George Adolphus Wigney's wife, married a Hannington.

Daniel Constable's diaries mention Robert several times and indicate that they were great friends. For example Daniel mentions a conversation in Wigney's drapery shop in about 1800, and describes a fight between them, lasting half an hour, after which they shook hands.

> *18 August 1798. Wigney and self quarreled, blows ensued, fought like tigers. He first tore my waistlet, then I his handkerchief, he again my handkerchief. Stopped half an hour after, shook hands and all was well.*

More significant, though, is their involvement in political reform and the establishment of a group of contacts amongst nonconformists in London, Brighton and Lewes, which would last all their lives.

We know from Daniel Constable's diaries that Robert mixed with this crowd, together with Charles Fleet (subsequently to edit the *Brighton Gazette* and write about the Wigneys in *Glimpses of Their Ancestors in Sussex*), Thomas West (the banker, who began as a clerk in Wigney's bank), Thomas Scutt (subsequently to make his fortune by developing Hove in his brickyard), Thomas Roff Tamplin (a Quaker who inherited a brewery behind the Bear Inn in Lewes, later a linen and woollen draper and clothier at 28 New Road, 'killed by the horns of a cow' in 1829), Thomas Cabell (Thomas Scutt's first cousin) and Billy and Bob (Robert) Williams. Charles Fleet called Robert 'a man of talent and energy'.[6]

This group attacked inherited privilege, the aristocracy and the power of the established church.

> *15 October 1799. Evening. Citizens Kennedy, Wilmshurst, Smith, Wigney and Turton went to the White Horse to take a social glass of generous wine. Turton sang 'Millions be Free'.*

Gypsy Bob, sporting at the time a Guildford address, subscribed to a book of Clio Rickman's poems in 1803.[7] Robert had probably left Brighton for Guildford in 1800.

31 January 1800. To Allens with West and Wigney to take our parting glass. 2 February 1800. Helped Wigney to pack trunks. 3 February 1800. R Wigney left Brighton. 2 March 1800. Got to Guildford, went to Mr Sparks thinking to find my friend Wigney there but was not so....writing to Wigney.

Incidentally, Daniel Constable's brother William later achieved special distinction after he moved back to Brighton around 1840. He bought a daguerrotype licence for £1000 and set himself up as a portrait photographer late in 1841. He achieved fame when he photographed Prince Albert, the Consort of Queen Victoria, for the first time in March 1842, after which he received Royal and Ducal patronage until his death in 1861.[8]

Robert Wigney had probably settled in Brighton by 1824 because he became a Brighton freemason then.[9] He is recorded as a lodging-house keeper at 10 Richmond Street, a house where George Adolphus Wigney had previously lived, in 1832.[10] An aggrieved local gentleman claimed that he himself should have been called 'Esquire' in a local directory, rather than a 'tradesman'. As an example, he said that Robert Wigney had been called 'Esq.' although he was really a lodging-house keeper. The magistrate responded by saying that most Esquires in Brighton let rooms.[11] Robert's involvement in so many local causes probably helped his nephew Isaac Newton Wigney to be elected in 1832, on a radical platform, as one of Brighton's first elected MPs.

He had been full of good works. In 1825, for example, he became a member of the inter-denominational 'Vestry Committee' of three parishioners, the vicar and his curate to investigate church wardens' accounts and arrears of church rates.[12] By 1830 he was chairman[13] and claiming that he did not see why the Church of England should hog all the money. He joined the committee of the Brighton Gas Light and Coke Company (with Thomas West and Thomas Scutt).[14] The following year he was in the chair and seeking to raise £30,000.[15] When Lord John Russell laid the foundation stone for the Royal British School in Edward Street in 1828, intended to be non-denominational to 'diffuse knowledge and education among the lower orders', Robert proposed three cheers and joined the Committee.[16] Other causes to attract his attention were support for the distressed manufacturers in Lancashire;[17] the Oriental Institute in Oriental Place;[18] the reconstitution of the damaged Chain Pier;[19] and the addition of fever wards to the Sussex County Hospital and Sea Bathing Infirmary.[20]

Later, he was attracted to overtly political matters. In 1829, he attended meetings[21] and joined committees[22] petitioning for the abolition of slavery. In 1831, when the King dissolved the parliament which had rejected the Reform Bill, Robert was one of the prime movers in arranging a meeting at the Old Ship Hotel to construct a petition to the King to thank him.[23] A Quaker cavilled at the proposed wording.

'Come forward', said Robert Wigney, 'like fighting men, and lay at the feet of your sovereign your purses and your lives' (tumultuous applause).

The Quaker was silenced. As national Political reform became topical, Robert joined a Brighton committee to prepare a petition to the House of Lords asking them to pass the Reform Bill.[24] It may be a little far fetched to trace the origins of Brighton's current radicalism – at the

time of writing it has Britain's only MP belonging to the
Green Party – to these years, but perhaps the seeds were
sown by a combination of men of principle and its high
proportion of religious nonconformists at that time.
Robert's brother William, too, donated to charitable
causes all his life.

After the election of Robert's nephew Isaac Newton as
an MP, there was a grand dinner in 1833 in a marquee in
Brown's Royal Gardens which nearly 600 local voters
attended.[25] Isaac Newton spoke, amid great cheering, and
so did George Faithfull, his fellow Brighton elected MP.
Robert may have gone a little too far when, towards the
end, he caused uproar with unsolicited comments on the
Corporation Bill.

> *If the bill introduced by the Lord Chancellor should pass
> into a law...we shall be exclusively governed by aristocrats
> and court sycophants. Until you get a Reform in the Church,
> your Reform in the State will be worth nothing; until you
> drive the Right Reverend Bench of Bishops from the
> Parliament of the United Kingdom, your reform will be
> good for nothing.*

So he was never afraid to speak up for his principles in
public.

In May 1834 Robert, in bed, felt unwell at midnight
and sought help from other members of his household.
They called for a doctor but he expired from a heart
attack.[26] He left specific sums of money to his widowed
sister, and her daughter, in Liverpool,[27] but brother
William was the executor and residuary legatee. William
returned the compliment in his own will, leaving the
residual sum to his own daughters, as he felt that Gypsy
Bob had intended.

6

GEORGE ADOLPHUS WIGNEY, THE FREE SPIRIT

EORGE ADOLPHUS, William's nephew, was an original and enterprising character who spent most of his life in Brighton, but at a considerable social distance from William the banker and his family. Born in Wakefield, the son of Joseph, William's younger brother, he entered William's life when he was tragically orphaned at the age of five and William took responsibility for him in Brighton. First, though, let us commemorate his parents, Joseph Wigney and Elizabeth, the third link, apart from William and Robert, with the weavers of the north.

Joseph is the ancestor of those in Britain, and many of those abroad, who still proudly bear the surname Wigney. The younger brother of William the Banker (Chapter 4) and the older brother of 'Gypsy Bob' (Chapter 5), he was the father of George Adolphus. Blessed with a happy marriage, he otherwise had a tough and tragic life.

Growing up on the family smallholding near Halifax, Joseph at first joined the 3rd Hussars.[1] In 1780, at the age of 20, he married Elizabeth Wyatt (b. 1762) in Manchester.[2] He and Elizabeth continued to have Manchester and Halifax connections all their lives. Three children were christened in Manchester, where Elizabeth's sister, nieces and nephews farmed at Moss

Side and Chetham's Hill. Joseph's mother Martha, and
Thomas III and John II, two of his brothers, continued to
live on the smallholdings at Skircoat, whilst William,
Joseph and ultimately Robert left home.

Out of the army, Joseph tried his luck as a general
trader in Bassinghall Street, Aldgate,[3] in central London.
This is the street where Weavers' Hall, the headquarters
of the Weavers Company, is located, and so perhaps he
was trading cloth from the north. The Land Tax records
for 1791 show him in Aldgate. But by 1793, he was
bankrupt.[4] In London, three of Joseph and Elizabeth's
children tragically died of smallpox. On the outbreak of
war in 1793, he signed up again to be a soldier, joining
the 22nd Dragoons. Frederick Charles (born 4 September
1793) was baptised at St Mary's, Newington, in
November 1793;[5] this is in Southwark, near Brixton and
the Elephant & Castle, so suggests that Elizabeth was in
south London at the time.

Joseph became a quartermaster and then a 2nd
lieutenant in the 22nd Dragoons. They were sent to
southern Ireland to help to quell a rebellion and to reduce
the opportunities of an invasion by the French from
Ireland. *Saunders' Newsletter* for 10 August 1795 tells
us: Died: at Bandon near Cork, Quartermaster Wigney 'in
consequence of a violent kick from his horse in an
exercise field'.[6] His wife Elizabeth, at 33 even younger,
died soon afterwards in London, it is said 'of a broken
heart' also in 1795. This orphaned their three surviving
children, John Wyatt Wigney (aged eleven), George
Adolphus Wigney (five) and Frederick Charles (two).

John Wyatt was of working age at the time, and joined
his relatives on one of the Manchester farms. He
remained in Manchester for the rest of his life. William's
nephew, George Adolphus (GA), moved to Brighton and
came under William's wing, with his younger brother

Frederick Charles. GA was to live even longer than William III and to spend the rest of his life in Brighton. He was original and rebellious, perhaps owing to his unsettled upbringing, and did not involve himself as much as his uncles and cousins in civic affairs. Instead of leaving Brighton when the bank crashed in 1842, he kept a low profile and stayed there until he died.

According to the memoir written about seventy years later by Frederick II, one of GA's sons,[7] William apparently sent both his nephews to be educated in France. This is puzzling, because Britain declared war on France in 1793, and the two nations were at loggerheads, on and off, until the Battle of Waterloo in 1815. William sent them both to be educated by a French Roman Catholic schoolmaster. At the time, in his Brighton house, William had four youngsters at home, his son Henry had recently died of infectious disease and his wife Ann was pregnant with Isaac Newton. Although, in the early years of the wars, England and France postured at one another across the English Channel, the Newhaven–Dieppe schooners still operated twice a week and trading across the Channel still took place.

When he returned, GA had a spell in the local militia and the Norfolk Regiment, but we can surmise that he did not find the discipline to his liking. He probably lived with William and his family, doing odd jobs around central Brighton in the coalyard, the brewery and the local shops, before moving to Chichester. There, involved in the import trade with Isigny, an agricultural town on the west coast of France, this moral, energetic young man, able to speak French, deeply read in science and respectful of Roman Catholicism, became a shrewd businessman.

At 9 North Street in Brighton, very close to the Castle, William's bank and the Steine, Thomas Wilmshurst was trading as a clockmaker, silversmith and jeweller. He was pursuing a well-established family tradition – indeed, his father Ninyon Wilmshurst (b. 1707) built a grandfather clock which is in the British Museum. Thomas's sister was married to a Hannington, who by then had taken over the drapers' shop nearby, which William had owned. The Wilmshursts were devoutly religious and probably descended from a German Protestant family. They had lodged with William when they first arrived in Brighton, and Thomas's 'merry little girl, with bright blue eyes, clear complexion, and curly hair as black as a raven, who could sing like a lark' had played with GA when they were young.

Naturally, GA's matrimonial thoughts turned towards Mary Ann Wilmshurst, his old playmate. He consulted his uncle. To his surprise, William opposed the match – after all, the Wilmshursts were only 'trade' who had accumulated a few hundred pounds; he expected his family to do better for themselves. This shows what a snob William had become in the 35 years since he turned up in Brighton with his 'donkey'.

George decided to marry for love, 'fully determined to fight the battle of life for himself', but he alienated William's family. By all accounts GA and Mary were very happy – they had ten children, who all survived to adulthood, in the next sixteen years – but William, annoyed, cut off financial support. We know all this because one of GA's sons, Frederick II, having emigrated to Australia and become a newspaper proprietor, left an autobiography, *The Past and the Present*, in which he described his origins in Brighton. This is the source of the quotations. In the end, William relented, leaving GA £400 when he died in 1836.

In his memoir Frederick paints a warm picture of an idiosyncratic childhood in Brighton in an extended family. For example, he was taken to see his great aunt.

I do not suppose any little boy or girl in South Australia has got such a big aunt as she was – she had become obese, obtuse and stone blind.... She used to be helped down stairs of a morning and helped upstairs again at night; and poor pussy was wont to sleep on her warm chair. Now I am going to relate a very sad tale as a warning to all naughty children who want to lay in bed too late. My big aunt was brought down stairs one morning as usual, and things went wrong all day. There was a grand holiday among the mice, and when that cat was called to do her duty, she was not present at her post; nor was the mystery revealed till it was time to remove my dear old aunt to her nocturnal rest; then that wicked cat, flattened out like a pancake, was found to have lost her nine lives, and perished in obscurity, all through not getting up early in the morning.

GA's marriage to Mary Wilmshurst, in 1814, when he was described as a grocer, had several important consequences. First, the descendants of this union include all the modern London and Oxford Wigneys, of which more later. Such were family sizes in those days that by the time he died, GA was a great-grandfather 40 times over. Second, echoes of Mary's evangelical religious beliefs resounded, within the family, down the next two centuries. Third, although many of GA's ultimate descendants had worthwhile careers and respectable professional jobs, they did not marry into moneyed families and the aristocracy like some of William's children. At first sight this might seem a disadvantage, but as we shall see, Isaac Newton Wigney and his sons and daughters got into all sorts of scrapes such as elopements, divorces, court cases – even murders. A moral sense may be a boon, even if accompanied by poverty. Fourth, with the benefit of hindsight, we can see this apparently minor family dispute as the origin of the situation in which, thirty or forty years later, in London, William's descendants were living the high life, whereas

GA's offspring and their children wallowed in poverty a few miles away.

Brewing

William's sons George, and William III, were several years older than George Adolphus. They took over the Wigney and Co. brewery in Ship Street. GA and his partner, grocers, were made bankrupt in Chichester in 1818.[8] Around 1820 Kemp Town, the area of densely packed Georgian boarding houses near the sea to the east of the Staithe, was starting to appear. In 1824 William III tried to establish a Black Rock brewery there with Thomas Reade Kemp, the developer, but this initiative soon failed. GA wished to become a brewer, but instead of using established brewing practices, he decided to work things out himself, from first principles, by starting a Kemp Town brewery. Despite the local involvement and investments of his cousins, characteristically, GA had branched out on his own without his uncle William's help. Judging by his attempt to sell the premises in 1831, his brewery was at 30 Richmond Buildings, though the office of the 'Royal Colonnade Brewery' was near the centre of Brighton at 5 New Road.[9]

At first GA did not have the slightest theoretical or practical knowledge. He paid someone for lessons, but all the tutor did was to carry out a few brews without explanation, pocket his fee and depart.

GA's first personal brew in 1818 turned out well and 'he thought himself a fine fellow'. A year passed in which he had managed to spoil several brews, filling the premises with stale beer, feeding his pigs on the rest and feeling less clever. The following year was disastrous. Descending into his new cleansing room one morning he was almost overcome by carbon monoxide gas; he added lime to neutralise it but abandoned the cleansing room.

> Malted some chick beans for curiosity; they absorbed so much water in the cistern, as to cause the charge of nearly or quite double duty. Mixed therewith some barley malt and brewed one guile, obtained but little extract, that was nauseous and spoiled the whole. Burnt down a malthouse by snapping porter malt on an improper kiln; killed a horse by feeding him on the half burnt barley and bean malt; by leaving on the cover of the manhole to wooden wort back over copper, while running off boiling wort into hop back, created a vacuum in the copper, and the pressure of the atmosphere broke the bottom of the back asunder, and forced it into the copper with a tremendous explosion....

Undaunted, he continued his experiments, and ultimately became a brewing expert.

Indeed, GA seemed determined to put the brewing of beer, ale and porter on a sounder scientific basis, using the principles of biology, chemistry and physics. Hitherto, it had been largely a craft activity, based on procedures handed down from one generation to the next, and subject to disasters if temperature markedly changed. He first produced in 1823 *A Philosophical Treatise on Malting and Brewing* (122 pp. with a glossary).[10] His second edition (nearly 300 pp.), *A Theoretical and Practical Treatise on Malting and Brewing* (1835), describes in detail his experiments on all aspects of the brewing process, with the aim of making it more efficient.

Before quantitative science was pursued, except in a few esoteric British and German universities, George Adolphus and his assistant, in a remote brewery in a small seaside town, were performing and analysing the results of experiments of international significance. This text, together with GA's *Elementary Dictionary or Cyclopaediae, for the Use of Maltsters, Brewers,*

Distillers, Rectifiers, Vinegar Manufacturers, and Others (1838) have become such classics that they are still in print, nearly 180 years later.[11]

Figure 6.1: One of George Adolphus Wigney's best-selling books, still in print nearly 200 years later.

GA's other interests

Around 1827 GA realised that when his mother Elizabeth died more than 30 years earlier, she may have left some money with her sister Catherine Chapman, living on a farm at Cheetham Hill in Manchester, which should have been his. So he petitioned the justices for the return of the money.[12] The detail in this document suggests that he, or members of his family such as his uncles William or Robert, must have remained in close touch with his Manchester relatives. Yet both Catherine Chapman, his aunt, and GA's brother John Wyatt, still living with her, wrote to tell him not to be so silly. We do not know the outcome of the case; perhaps finances were tight, for he put his Richmond Street brewery up for sale by auction in 1831.[13]

GA also put his original mind to use in designing a new harbour for Brighton to make it more of a commercial port. He published this in the *Mechanics Magazine* in 1842.

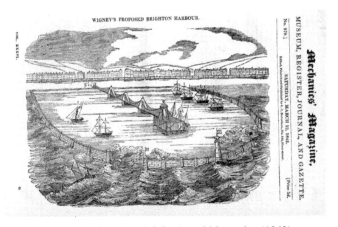

Figure 6.2: George Adolphus's ambitious plan (1842)
for a new harbour at Brighton.

The local fishing fleet had drastically declined because of the demands of those visiting Brighton for sea bathing, pleasure and frippery. It was impossible for large cargo ships to unload speedily at Brighton. Although the Chain Pier (erected 1823, storm-damaged 1833, burnt down 1896) was far ahead of its time, larger steam-vessels were now being built and by 1842 Southampton had taken away from Brighton the important cross-channel steam-packet trade.

GA's proposal was for a massive concrete breakwater encased in iron plates, over a quarter of a mile long. He suggested tunnels leading northwards beneath the town, from West Street to the new railway yards (the railway had reached Brighton in 1841), so that goods could be transported to and from the harbour and the railway. His proposal did not attract much local support. Although a sheltered harbour with loading bays made plenty of business sense, it would have devastated tourism. In the end, Shoreham and Newhaven attracted, instead, even the smaller vessels.

Very little was heard of George Adolphus between the Wigney bank's collapse in 1842 and his death in 1872. The census returns show that he remained in Brighton, like at least three of his children. In the town directory (1848) he is described as a wine merchant and general trader operating from 24 New Road, with son Frederick as a printer; next door at 23 New Street, his daughter Catherine is a milliner and straw bonnet maker. His last will is written from 2 Church Street, where he died in 1872 at the age of 82.

This group of handsome Grade II-listed cobble-fronted buildings, on the corner of Church Street and New Street, (Figure 6.3) was built as the Regent Hotel in 1807 after New Street, near the Brighton Pavilion, had been established in 1804-06. Uncle William owned it when he made his will in 1835. By the time George Adolphus died he obviously owned this complex, because in his will his executors were instructed to sell it for not less than £1800.[14] Perhaps he bought it with the £400 Uncle William left him when he died in 1836.

Occasionally, GA gave his children money when they were desperate. Times for them were tough, however, and six of them eventually emigrated to Australia or Canada.

Figure 6.3: The elegant Grade II listed houses in a prominent position in New Road/Church Street in Brighton, owned by George Adolphus Wigney. They were built as the Regency Hotel. Daughter Catherine was the proprietor of the milliner's shop next to the church.

George Adolphus's wife Mary died in about 1856. GA married again, to Anna Maria Constantine. GA must have left a memoir, which we have not found, because his son Frederick II refers to it in 1885. In view of what happened to the major Wigneys in Brighton in 1842, however, it is not surprising that the relatives of Isaac Newton Wigney kept a low profile. It is striking that whilst many of GA's children were eking out a living in the poorest part of London, as we describe in Chapters 14 and 15, their great uncle William had become the equivalent of a multi-millionaire and their second cousins, the children of Isaac Newton Wigney, were mixing with the aristocracy, and marrying them, in Belgravia, despite their father's misdemeanours.

7

FREDERICK CHARLES's MENTAL HEALTH

ILLIAM WIGNEY'S WILL, written in 1835, left £400 to his nephew George Adolphus.[1] This must have come as a welcome surprise to GA, who had fallen out with his uncle twenty years earlier and appears to have been financially challenged all his life. But William left nothing to GA's brother Frederick Charles.[2] Perhaps he did not even know what had happened to Frederick, after he had sponsored the orphan boy, aged just over 15, to leave London as third mate on the *Helen Elle* on 30 December 1808, destined to join the Indian Army as a cadet.[3]

Trade with India, and China, and the activities of the East India Company, which had the monopoly at the time, were crucial to Britain.[4] Its hundreds of ships exported textiles, iron, muskets and other goods, and imported cotton, silk, indigo, salt, saltpetre (potassium nitrate, essential to make gunpowder), tea and opium. Its trading interests were at first protected by its own troops, and despite the need to employ so many troops in the Napoleonic Wars in Europe, large regiments of British troops were simultaneously involved in India, based in Calcutta (Bengal), Madras and Bombay, where they fought one war after another to subdue the India maharajahs. Some regiments trained and employed sympathetic native Indian troops, such as the 15th Regiment of the Bengal native infantry, which Frederick Charles joined. He was an Ensign at the age of 16 on 22 October 1808, and a second lieutenant in the 2nd battalion by 15 May 1814, at the age of 21. Perhaps William Wigney paid for his commission.

The most significant war around that time was the third Anglo-Maratha War (1817–18), which employed over 120,000 troops in British regiments in the Bengal Army, and finally subdued most of India under British Rule. It seems likely that Frederick Charles fought in this war. But on 19 June 1819, at the age of 26, he was invalided out of the British Army. Yet he was not repatriated for another six years.

At that time regiments in India supported a substantial number of camp followers, 'wives' and children. Some of these had emigrated with their husbands and some had appeared as part of the 'fishing fleet', the boatloads of well-off young women who travelled to India each year in an effort to find a suitable military husband.[5] Many soldiers, however, mixed with the Indian aristocracy or acquired native wives. This practice began to be frowned upon and legislated against from 1795 onwards. Nevertheless, it still continued amongst the lower ranks, and in outlying districts. Whilst there are no records of a marriage, it seems likely that Frederick Charles 'married' a native Indian lady, perhaps in a Sikh ceremony. They had four daughters, Ann Eliza (born 1818 in Cawnpore but died very young?), Jane Eliza, Rose and Caroline (later Charlotte). We have some records of their births, baptisms and marriages, and they gave rise to families of their own in India, the Aviets and the Dodsworths.[6] But it was not the policy at the time to transport native Indian 'wives' back to Britain with their husbands. So Frederick Charles probably travelled back alone, leaving a pregnant wife behind. But by that time, he had a psychiatric illness.[7]

Ann Eliza Wigney was born on 2 September 1818 at Cawnpore, to Lt and Mrs Wigney. Under age, she married Gentloom Aviet, an Armenian interpreter to Sir John Grant, in June 1834 in Calcutta Cathedral. Unfortunately he only lived a couple of years, until September 1836. Meanwhile, however, their daughter Georgiana Frederika Wigney Aviet was born in Calcutta ten months after they married, and their son Gentloom Charles Adolphus Aviet was born in May 1837.

Rose Wigney's date of birth is uncertain, but she married William Thompson Dodsworth, of the revenue survey department in Calcutta, in January 1842. She is described as a 'ward of the military orphan institute', so perhaps her mother had died, or perhaps the military took responsibility for Frederick Charles's wife and children after Frederick Charles was repatriated. Their son George Wigney Dodsworth was born at Cawnpore, India, on 22 April 1845. Some of his Dodsworth descendants became established in Britain. So perhaps Frederick Charles still has descendants and extant fragments of DNA. Eliza and Rose's sister, Charlotte, was born in 1826 in India after Frederick had travelled back to England. He probably never saw her. She was unmarried, dying in Dinapore, India in 1898, aged 72.

Frederick Charles spent the rest of his life, from 1825 to 1852, at Pembroke House in Hackney, a home for those with mental problems invalided out of the Indian armies. His death certificate (17 April 1852) states the cause of death as 'dementia thirty years, general decline one month'. Even at that time, facilities for those who had suffered shell-shock and similar injuries during war were sophisticated. In 1844 Pembroke House hosted '95 lunatics' who seemed to be sensitively treated, employed in various trades and frequently rehabilitated.[8]

> Although Pembroke House was not the only institution in Britain to receive patients who were transferred from the three Indian asylums to the east, it nevertheless provided for the majority of formally institutionalized returned expatriates. By 1892 about 500 lunatics who had claim on being maintained by the company had passed through the asylum in England.

There are many questions here to which we shall probably never know the answers. What was the nature of Frederick's illness? Was it the result of a physical injury or might it have been shell-shock? An indication comes in a letter from his brother George Adolphus. He mentions a bright light which caused Frederick to fall off his horse. Perhaps an epileptic fit caused a stroke? Where did he live in India in the six years it took to repatriate him? Were his wife and daughters with him during that time?

During his spell in Pembroke House, Fred was probably totally unaware of his uncle William's death in 1836 and the dramatic events unfolding in Brighton as his cousin, Isaac Newton Wigney MP, was mentally hung, drawn and quartered after the collapse of the Wigney Bank.

8

ISAAC NEWTON WIGNEY
& THE BANK CRASH

W E DO NOT KNOW what possessed William and
Ann to name their second surviving son Isaac
Newton (INW); perhaps this reflected his
parent's agreement with Isaac Newton's religious views,
critical of orthodox Christianity. Or perhaps they were
following Clio Rickman (see Chapter 4, p. 50), who had
given each of his six sons Christian names which were
surnames of famous people whom he admired – Paine,
Washington, Franklin, Rousseau, Petrarch and Volney.
INW was born at Brighthelmston on 10 March 1795, at
1550 on a Tuesday afternoon. His rather grandiose and
distinctive Christian names seem appropriate for
someone who, one way or another, made a national
impact.

We can imagine INW growing up in the centre of town
at a time when it was at its Regency zenith. The Prince
Regent and Mrs Fitzherbert spent most of their time just
over the road or round the corner. Regency toffs, their
wives, families and servants, patronised the local shops
and his fathers bank, there were frequent parties, concerts
and balls, whole families liked to be seen promenading
along the Staithe. Society had an underbelly too, a
maelstrom of soldiers, grooms and tarts, who patronised
the family public houses and bought their beer.

All this must have rubbed off on INW, who was probably tutored with friends from families higher up the social scale, and adopted some of the manners and social habits of the upper class. Soon after William moved to Hassocks in 1811, INW was riding to hounds with his friends. His father, and brother George the brewer, both Commissioners, probably entertained aristocratic guests at Newtimber House. INW probably began to involve himself in the Brighton social scene, and to meet his acquaintances in London, linked to Lewes and Brighton by frequent horse-drawn coach services.

By his early twenties, INW was working part-time in his father's bank, with a view to ultimately taking over. His older brothers William III and George were by then involved in the breweries. Clement, ultimately destined to help in the bank, was five years younger than INW.

INW spent more and more of his time in London. Eventually, in 1825, he married the beauty Caroline Walter, and set up home in London. Caroline came from a wealthy well-connected family and her grandfather, having established *The Times* newspaper, had been its first editor.[1] Her father William edited *The Times* from 1800 to 1803. Her uncle, John Walter II, afterwards established *The Times* on a sound commercial basis, introducing technology into printing via the steam press in 1814.

John Walter II was a formidable character; for example when William Pitt, resentful of *The Times'* exposure of Melville, arranged for all correspondence addressed to the newspaper to be intercepted at Gravesend, John Walter II organised smugglers to pick up dispatches from French boats; as a result, *The Times* reported the Battle of Trafalgar before the Government! Eventually, in 1832, JWII joined INW as an MP. Caroline's family built Bearwood House, one of the largest nineteenth-century brick houses, and owned the *The Times* newspaper until

1908. For the fourth generation in succession, the pattern of Wigney men marrying wives from well-established and well-off families was repeated.

By the late 1820s, William was in his early seventies and INW and Clement were largely organising the Brighthelmstone Bank themselves, in INW's case, from a distance. In charge of day-to-day business was Mr Hartstone, so dependable that he was left a legacy in William's will. Because of the building work associated with the building of the Brighton Pavilion, the bank's premises had moved to 60 East Street, still very much in the social whirl of the main shopping centre. Clement bought the house next door to live in, but INW was the senior partner.

INW was not only a Town Commissioner, but a local magistrate and the first Treasurer of the Brunswick Square Commissioners (1830).[2] At first though (at least in 1823–28) he lived in the newly built Regency Square, in Kemp Town.

The Reform Act of 1830 created universal suffrage for men. So for the first time, Brighton residents and householders were able to vote for representation in Parliament. Because of its explosive growth, the population of Brighton merited two MPs. INW decided to stand, and for the first time appeared on the hustings as a Whig with Radical sympathies.

Of course, he and his family were particularly well-known in Brighton, where they had a strong and reliable reputation. In 1832, INW was elected after topping the poll as one of Brighton's first two MPs elected on the basis of universal suffrage. Some impression of the importance which the local population attached to the hustings is provided by the scenes outside the Town Hall when he was nominated as an MP for the third time in 1841 (see lithograph, Figure 8.1).

Figure 8.2: The scene outside Brighton Town Hall in 1841, at the hustings, on the day when Isaac Newton Wigney was nominated as an MP. The vast attendance shows the importance the local population attached to being able to elect their MPs.

Figure 8.2: Isaac Newton Wigney MP, from a painting
of all the MPs in the 1832–36 session of Parliament.

He lost the next election in 1837, partly because some
of the locals felt that his sophisticated airs and graces
were unjustified in view of his humble origins. He was
ridiculed afterwards because his 'important and valuable
services lie rendered to the country, and the world
generally, during his parliamentary career', in an
extraordinary but brilliant piece of lampoonery in the
Brighton Patriot (21 November 1837). The Whigs
intended to present him with a piece of plate; perhaps the
most appropriate form would be a 'silver beer barrel of
large dimensions, supported on the shoulders of a giant.
The beer barrel would be typical of the source from

whence the wealth of the Wigney family sprung, and the giant would demonstrate the vast overwhelming power of that family.' Isaac Newton's projected reply at the presentation included the comment that 'I promise you, gentlemen, that no member will walk through the lobby and drink a glass of negus and smoke a cigar in the coffee-house with more assiduity than myself.'

Isaac Newton and Caroline lived in Porchester Place in London, where they brought up six surviving children, most of whom led fascinating lives (see later). We imagine that he neglected his father's creation, the bank in Brighton, by now called Wigney & Co.

But he managed to retake his parliamentary seat in 1841 to great acclaim, by regaining the populist vote. A report on a meeting in 1841 to promote his candidature was attended by about 300 local tradesmen, the basis of his support. They came from the gentlemen of the urban middle classes, besides butchers, bakers, painters and bricklayers entitled to vote as a result of the 1832 Reform Act. His various speeches, reported verbatim in the *Brighton Herald*, are rather vacuous and long-winded. As an MP he was not particularly distinguished. This time, however, he only represented Brighton for a year, and the local tradesmen who supported him in the election were those hardest hit by the collapse of his bank.

On 4 March 1842, a notice appeared on the door of the bank in East Street, apologising for its closure: 'Messrs Wigney and Co. deeply regret the painful necessity of suspending their payments.'[3] A few days earlier, Sir Henry Wheatley had apparently deposited £10,000 on behalf of Queen Victoria.[4] According to *The Times*, a depositor testified that on the previous day, 'he saw Mr Clement Wigney at the bank, apparently in a great passion, and throwing the books about the office'.

Two days after the collapse, *The Times* reported that 'Every hour brings us acquainted with some new instance in which tradesmen have lost large sums of money, which will cripple or entirely destroy their business.'

An account of the consequences, by Charles Fleet in 1885, suggests that the Wigneys in Brighton 'came from nowhere, sprang up like mushrooms, and suddenly declined, so that now there is not a single Wigney left in Brighton'. The impact was dramatic, if not quite on the scale of the recent collapses of Lehman Brothers, Lloyds TSB or Black Rock.

It emerged that in the previous weeks, INW had been frantically trying to raise funds in London to support the bank. Ultimately he had to admit defeat. The background to the case was exposed to public view in a series of bankruptcy trials in 1842 in which INW was mercilessly cross-examined by one of the most aggressive lawyers of the day.[5] These trials took place at Brighton Assizes in full view of the local creditors, and received thorough newspaper coverage, even in *The Times*, owned by INW's wife's family. Investors turned up in force to hear in detail why they had lost virtually all their money; in the end, they only received a shilling in the pound although George paid back the £4,800 owed to the Town Council. Even when William died in 1836 the bank had been technically insolvent; as the Commissioner pointed out at Clement's bankruptcy hearing, if the bank had been closed immediately on William's death, as stipulated in his will, the shortfall would have been £50,000 rather than £120,000.

INW was forced to apply for the Chiltern Hundreds and had to resign his parliamentary seat. As Charles Fleet dramatically puts it, 'He was ... being killed by inches'.

Eyewitnesses of the court proceedings:

looking back on that scene, and recalling that pale, haggard, scared but once handsome, if weak face – knowing that his nature was a kind and gentle one – knowing that he loved and was proud of his wife and doted on his son – remembering that he had been, during the whole of his life, petted by his father, and looked up to by every Wigney as the pride of the family – remembering....what he had to endure as he stood there to explain and justify acts which could not be explained or justified, and that his questioner was the legal bully of Brighton – we can feel pity for the man....[6]

Afterwards, stressed and in poor health, he returned as a bankrupt to Porchester Place, where he died on 8 February 1844, at the age of 49. His wife, of course, had 'private means' but she became peripherally involved in the trials.

In 1837 INW's credit with men of standing had been damaged by his appearance as a witness at the notorious De Ros trial,[7] which involved cheating at cards at Graham's Club and discredited several people in the highest social circles. This suggested that INW had become used to an extravagant style of living. In fact it emerged later, at the trial, that his lifestyle cost £2,600 a year and that he had been playing whist for high stakes.

The bank's difficulties, however, went far deeper than this. INW had been well aware of the potential problem when he was re-elected an MP a year earlier. In fact, for three years, he had been living on 'hope deferred which maketh the heart sick', 'suffering tortures both of body and mind, such as can scarcely be conceived'. It emerged that INW had been using the money deposited in the bank in a series of ill-judged speculations, in particular in the manufacture of fine cloth made from merino wool in Glasgow.

Charles Cochrane, who some regarded as 'slightly cracked', invested in machinery in Glasgow in the early 1830s to make cloth from the wool of merino sheep of higher quality than that made by the French at the time. Although Cochrane died in 1834, the factory continued to operate. Stimulated by conversations with two fellow MPs, and with his father's initial approval, in the early 1830s INW began to invest some of his bank's money in the enterprise. Altogether, Mr James the prosecutor alleged,[8] INW advanced £73,000 of the bank's money over the years. Isaac claimed that he had tried to extract himself from the enterprise in 1834, but was continually hoodwinked. When he visited Glasgow twice a year, he was reassured that Holdsworth's factory, as it was now called, was doing well, and that it would yield profits in the end. He put James Young, who had married his older sister Mary Anne, in charge in 1838, but this seemed to have no impact.

INW's defence was unconvincing, since the Wigney Bank's financial return from the enterprise over the years amounted to zero, and the bank had not produced formal accounts since 1824. He had destroyed much of the correspondence with the Glasgow enterprise. His brother Clement knew of a debt, but had no concept of its scale.

Mr Bennett:	*Have you ever been solvent since 1836?*
INW:	*Certainly not, considering the scale of my operations.*
Mr Bennett:	*Can you fix a period when the bank was solvent?*
INW:	*Immediately on my father's death.*

This was in 1836 and before William's will had been proved and his assets distributed, many to his daughters.[8]

Quite apart from this, INW had invested unwisely in an India rubber factory, and in 1840, in a potato sugar manufactory in St George's-in-the-East, London, a 'horrible vortex' into which he invested £8285 for a return of £730. Some of the money he used for this venture probably came from brother George who, although not directly involved in the administration of the bank, had no illusions about its financial prospects. In 1840 George had bought his three brothers, INW, Clement and William III out of the family brewery for £10,000 each, and loaned the bank another £10,000.[9] This undoubtedly kept the bank afloat for longer.

During the bankruptcy hearings, INW was repeatedly questioned about personal property which he might have hidden from his creditors. These allegations were never proved, but they strongly hinted at dishonesty. For example, why was his Adelaide Street house in Brighton now furnished so simply, with hardly any wine, silver or books around? There were not even pillows on the beds. Why did his wife send various parcels to London in the year before the bank collapsed?[10]

On the day after the bank closed, 5 March, a horse-drawn brewery cart had drawn up outside isaac's Adelaide Street house. It was loaded by the servants with boxes of personal effects, which were then deposited in the hay-loft of his brother George's brewery in Ship Street. Other boxes were sent to London by train. A letter from INW's wife to George was tabled. With it, she sent him a key to one of the boxes, and asked him to take out a silver salver and some pictures and keep them in one of his closets. This should be done '*without a second person knowing about it*' since it is '*so necessary to be quiet on this occasion, and I hope that it will be done in the evening to avoid observation*'.

The atmosphere was heightened when it emerged in the final days of the trial that there were still undeclared assets at the bank premises, such as gold coins and share certificates.

Figure 8.3: Caricature: 'The man who broke the bank in Brighton Town'.

INW, who was warned that the penalty for non-disclosure of assets was transportation, and Clement were sent with court officers to collect them. For example, at the last gasp Clement collected £50 in notes and £200 in gold from the bank, admitting that he had sent boxes of goods and chattels to his wife's father and a friend by rail to London, and divulged that he had capital in three houses in Brighton. With this the hearing was finally adjourned, 'leaving the creditors and all the town amazed at these seeming attempts at evasion'. Boxes of goods and chattels from London destined for the court subsequently arrived at Brighton railway station.

In retrospect, it seems likely that the Wigney Bank was doomed in the long run. Despite its small size, there were seven banks in Brighton in 1800, but only two survived by 1840. After the Wigney bank crash, the single remaining bank became part of Barclays in 1895. The death knell of local country banks was the coming of the railways, which produced a demand for money on a national scale. Yet the Bankruptcy Commissioners in 1842 exposed the situation in which, from about the date at which he had first been elected to Parliament, INW had been using depositors' money to invest in a speculative enterprise 500 miles away which had little prospect of success. The Bank Charter Act of 1844, which restricted the issue of new bank notes to the Bank of England, must have been partly stimulated by this debacle.

Isaac Newton and Clement were made bankrupt. INW was made to resign as treasurer to the Brighton Commissioners, a post which he had taken over from his brother George. Clement sold his house in Oriental Place. It may have been at this juncture that George Adolphus took over his Regent Hotel, at 2 Church Street and 23 & 24 New Street. Despite their previous reputation as pillars of the local community, the Wigney family name in Brighton was mud. Even the bank premises were demolished. Isaac Bass bought the building soon afterwards to provide an approach to East Street and the Town Hall from the Old Steine.

During INW's brief occupation of his palatial house at 1 Adelaide Terrace in Brighton in 1841–42, there was a quotation over the front door *Vix ea nostro voco* (I scarcely call these things my own). This caused much amusement at the trial.[11]

INW only lasted for a couple of years after the trial. He died on 8 February 1844, after years of ill-health and months of severe suffering. But he 'left a numerous family'. We shall explore their exploits later.

Yet George and William III had stuck to brewing. Relatively untainted, they continued to run the Wigney brewery in Brighton. After George's death at Barcombe in 1847,[12] brother William III took over the brewery, but this Ship Street Brewery and all the 87 associated public houses and land were sold in 1850 before his death. The advertisement[13] suggested that it 'may truly be designated one of the most lucrative and eligible concerns within 60 miles of London' and that 'The great celebrity of "Wigney's Entire" commands an extensive trade.'[14]

In retrospect, looking back over the previous 25 years, it is difficult to value William's estate (1836).[15] Contemporary commentators have produced conflicting estimates. William appeared rich and lived in pomp. He owned banks, breweries and public houses, and had many other investments. The goodwill alone must have been worth a great deal. Yet, was there a long-term deficit stemming from the difficulties that all banks faced in 1825, and when he distributed money willy-nilly at that stage (Chapter 3), did he create debts? A debt of £9,000 was suggested at the bankruptcy trial. Was the bank's money subsequently being used to shore up mortgages and pay the interest on loans? Did this stimulate William's request to his sons in his will, which they ignored, to sort out the bank's finances, and by implication, to start again? Did INW already know that there was a problem when he first stood for Parliament in 1832? We shall never know.

Two sets of enterprising Wigneys still existed, however: the sophisticates and the paupers.

The sophisticates were INW's children, four daughters aged eleven to sixteen and two sons aged eighteen and nine, immersed in London society with a very rich mother.

The relative paupers were of the same generation, the offspring of INW's cousin George Adolphus Wigney and his wife Mary Ann Wilmshurst in Brighton. They eventually ended up all over Britain and the Commonwealth, and became lost in the vast throng of life. First we shall explain the fascinating exploits of the young family INW left behind, and then, in the final part of the book, discuss the efforts of GA's descendants to make a living.

PART III

ISAAC NEWTON
WIGNEY'S FAMILY

9

CLARENCE IN LOVE?

OW DID Isaac Newton Wigney's children fare after his death in London in 1844? It seems likely that they themselves were hardly affected by the bankruptcy, which soon faded into obscurity. Brighton, and their remaining Brighton relatives, must have seemed a world away. INW's wife, Caroline, was rich in her own right and lived in a palatial house in Devonshire Square in the midst of Victorian London society. Her children were presented at court[1] and the girls became debutantes. Her sons moved in the social set of Eton and the Guards.

Let us begin with their oldest child, Clarence. After Eton,[2] Clarence joined the army and was sent to India with the East India Company. As a lieutenant, in early 1848 at the age of 22, he was presented at Court on his return from his first spell of Indian duty. By 1850, aged 24, Clarence was a captain in the 58th Native Infantry, serving near Mooltan in India, when he married Louisa Hoghton. Between these two excursions to India he was involved in a caddish escapade which scandalised London society and even reached the House of Lords. For Louisa had been married before, to Henry (Bold-) Hoghton.

Henry was the eldest son of Sir Henry Hoghton Bart, of Hoghton Towers in Lancashire. At the age of 21, the younger Henry inherited a substantial Lancashire estate. Early that year, in 1842, he met Louisa Josephine Saunders, then only 17 but 'possessed of great personal

attractions'.[3] He was smitten, and in June 1842, he
followed her to Boulogne, proposed marriage, and was
accepted. Her mother advised against the responsibility
of an immediate union. In the meantime, Henry settled on
Louisa substantial funds. They were married at St
George's, Hanover Square in August 1845.

After a honeymoon on the Continent lasting several
months, the couple moved into an estate Henry had
bought in Hafod, Cardigan, from the Duke of Lancaster,
where they lived 'in great affection', happily entertain-
ing relatives. In the spring of 1848, they moved into
London hotels whilst their Welsh property was
renovated.

On 9 April 1848, Louisa went to Greenwich with a
friend, the wife of the MP for Montgomeryshire, and by
chance met Clarence. He had missed an appointment, and
they asked him to join their party instead. The Chartist
riots in London were the following day, and Henry and
Clarence were driven around London to follow the
action.

A week later Henry was called away to Hafod to assess
the renovations, but after three weeks or so he returned to
London where he, his manservant Hirst, Louisa and her
maid stayed at Milvert's hotel (now Claridge's). On
Wednesday 21 June 1848, after Louisa's maid had gone
to Bristol, Hirst drove Louisa to a friend's house in
Langham Place for tea. On his return, he discovered that
Henry's dinner appointment with Sir Archibald M'Clay
was for the following night, not that night as Louisa had
told Henry. Suspicious, he went to Louisa's room, where
'on looking around he missed the various articles which
usually comprise the requirements for a ladies toilet, and
also a box'. He and Henry soon found some letters which
confirmed the intimacy between Clarence and Louisa.
Perhaps they had eloped.

Figure 9.1: A more mature Louisa at the time of her third marriage.

From the indignant Henry's point of view, as expressed by his counsel at the subsequent action for damages,[4] Clarence 'had so woven his chain around the unhappy woman, that he was soon afterwards enabled to carry her off, never to return to that home and happiness she had once enjoyed'. Or perhaps, as Clarence's counsel suggested, his client was 'a young man, only 23 years of age, who had yielded to a sudden temptation'.

Clarence and Louisa had met in Kensington Gardens, Regent's Park and at the London Zoo, but Hirst had not mentioned his suspicions in case they were ill-founded and made Henry and Louisa unhappy. He and a policeman called Ledbetter ultimately traced Clarence and Louisa to Weisbaden on the Rhine, where they were living as 'Mr and Mrs Wilmott'. They had taken the train to Dover, and then passed through Ostend and Brussels on the way. After a couple of months, 'Mr and Mrs Wilmott' returned to lodge in London, from where, on 20 October 1848, they embarked to India. In those days it took months to sail to India, but Louisa wrote from Calcutta on 21 December.

In that letter she confirmed that she was pregnant and was expecting to be confined in late February, after which she would join Clarence at his Regiment. It appears from Henry's incensed action for damages, in January 1849, that he felt that the child was his. His counsel explained that

> Mrs Hoghton was now in the family way by her husband, and in a few short months the union would have been strengthened by the birth of a child. What were now the prospects of the child? Hearts warmed with love would have received it, but now the hands of a guilty mother would be the first to hold it, and its first home would be amidst guilt and shame.[5]

But can we be sure? The child could have been conceived in late May, when Clarence and Louisa were seeing one another. So Louisa eloped with Clarence Wigney on 21 June barely knowing that she was pregnant. How did Henry find out about the pregnancy?

Why would you elope in the early stages of pregnancy with your husband's child? Louisa must have been desperate to leave Henry and be with Clarence.

In those days, wives were still regarded as their husband's possessions. In the Sheriff's Court in London January 1849, Henry sued the absent Clarence for £10,000, a million pounds in today's money, for stealing his wife. Both Henry's and Clarence's counsels pointed out that that adultery was not a crime. Clarence's solicitor argued that Henry was so rich that he would not notice any damages he received, but a major settlement would keep his client in exile for life or expose him to permanent imprisonment if he returned to Britain. The jury retired for 15 minutes and awarded Henry £3,000 rather than the £10,000 he had requested.

Louisa gave birth to a son on 5 February 1849 in Kolrata, Bengal, India. He was named Cecil Bold-Hoghton. Throughout his life he was called Cecil de Houghton or just Cecil Hoghton, and was the only son which Henry 'fathered'.

Subsequent hearings in the House of Lords in March 1849 decided that because of proof of adultery or Clarence and Louisa's absence in India, a divorce could go ahead. The Lords granted the divorce in July 1849, son Cecil was christened on 23 October, and Clarence and Louisa married at Lahore by special licence on 30 October.

Yet they had barely been married a month when tragedy struck. On 2 December, Clarence died of typhus, at the age of 24. What a disaster, after all the sacrifices that he and Louisa had made to be together!

Louisa rapidly returned to London, and wasted no time. In March 1851 she married another well-connected military man, Edmund Henry St. John Mildray, son of the MP for Winchester, Sir Henry St John Carew St John

Mildray (4th baronet). Living at the family seat at Dogmersfield in Hampshire, she had three children before her death at the age of 40. Meanwhile her original husband became the 9th de Hoghton baronet in 1862, and began the restoration of the derelict Hoghton Towers into the striking Grade 1 Elizabethan fortified manor house which is such a popular visitor attraction today.

No doubt Henry had been angry and aggrieved at losing his wife to the son of a bankrupt banker. Yet he continued to support 'his' son. Cecil was sent to Harrow, and in the register is down as the son of H. Hoghton Esq. When he left in 1862, he was only aged thirteen. His next appearance is in the 1871 census, when he was lodging in a house in St Hellier, Jersey as a married man with Charlotte de Hoghton, whom we assume was his wife, although there is no record of their marriage. Cecil died in Brussels on 24 July 1871, aged just 25.

We must applaud the integrity of the press. The details of these trials and tribulations are all recorded in *The Times*, at a time when the family of Clarence's mother, Caroline (Walter), owned the newspaper.

10

CONSTANCE'S MARRIAGE, PATRICK'S ESCAPADES & THE ARDLAMONT 'MURDER' MYSTERY

HEN CONSTANCE, aged 21, the oldest of Isaac Newton and Caroline's daughters, was the first to marry in 1851, she probably felt secure.[1] Her new husband, an Irish aristocrat, was Loftus Abraham Algernon Tottenham, High Sherriff of Leitrim, in Antrim. His father was related to the Marquis of Ely, his mother was an heiress, the niece of the Earl of Erne, and five of his immediate ancestors had been MPs. When Constance's only son was born five years later, he was christened Beresford Patrick Creighton-Stuart Loftus Tottenham.[2] Not only was this a mouthful, but he proved to be a handful. This grandson of Isaac Newton Wigney (INW) turned out to be an unreliable but plausible rogue, whose CV included a major supporting role in the 'Ardlamont murder'. For convenience let us call him Patrick, or PLT.

Patrick took the usual route for INW's grandsons into the army, emerging briefly in 1877, at the age of 21, as a lieutenant in the 10th Hussars. Even by that time he was £3,000 in debt, perhaps equivalent to £200,000 today; he never cleared it. To avoid facing the music, he became a mercenary. He served as a captain in the Turkish army for four years, then spent a year in Greece and another in

Venezuela. His ten military years probably taught him to overcome hardship and stand up for himself. Perhaps his subsequent dealings sometimes required strong-arm tactics.

Figure 10.1: Beresford Patrick Creighton-Stuart Loftus Tottenham: a sketch made at the Edinburgh trial in 1894.[3]

After selling wine on commission, Patrick returned to London in 1886, at the age of 30, to become a 'financial agent' without any capital. As he admitted later, 'his business consisted of obtaining loans on reversions of doubtful value and other securities of an indifferent character'. He moved around and changed the name of his practice, presumably to avoid creditors. He began as 'Montague Tottenham' at 57 Lincoln's Inn Fields, soon moving to Great James Street and then to Chancery Lane by 1890, all addresses with kudos. A year later he was Kempton & Co. (perhaps a subliminal reference to Brighton) in Delahaye Street, Westminster, moving to Cockspur Street by 1894. Later, he tried trading as Lofthouse & Co. from his flat at 2 Marylebone Mansions, near Victoria Street, and as 'Charles O'Malley' in Piccadilly. By that time, he was not only avoiding creditors, but finding it difficult to attract custom because of his involvement in the Ardlamont murder and subsequent trials in early 1894.

In 1899 PLT was officially bankrupted, with assets of £3,000 but liabilities of £10,000.[4] The following year, he was a witness in a divorce case in which he prevented one of his clients from throwing his wife, seeking divorce, over the banisters.[5] His application to be discharged in 1910 met with the following response. . Refused. He had omitted to keep proper books of account, continued to trade knowing himself to be insolvent and contributed to his bankruptcy by rash and hazardous speculations and unjustifiable extravagance in living. In 1905, still trading under the name 'Lubbock', he was convicted of obtaining a loan without revealing that he was an un-discharged bankrupt. When his creditors met on 19 August 1915 to discuss a receiving order, Patrick claimed that the First World War prevented him from repaying them from assets in Germany.

Finance, however, did not take up all PLT's time. An unmarried local music teacher, Maud Francis Daniell had a son in 1897. He was named Beresford Loftus Edward Daniell Tottenham. Beresford was probably farmed out to a wet nurse, because he died of dehydration and rickets at 14 months in one of the poorest districts of London. When we told Maud's family, they were shocked, because they always assumed that she had died a maiden lady.

In 1902 Patrick, at 46, married Emily Bannester, apparently aged 22, in Brighton. From the other records of her life, such as her death certificate, it seems most likely that she was only 19 at the time she married, below legal age.[6] They had no recorded children. After PLTs death in 1929 she married a Frenchman pretty quickly.

Patrick's father, aged about 90, was living with him in his London flat in the 1901 census, when Patrick is recorded as a clerk. Perhaps his father at first, or Emily later, supported PLT financially.

All these events were mere pinpricks compared to the impact of the Ardlamont mystery on Patrick's life. After the high profile of the sensational trial in early 1894, and the subsequent actions, he became notorious. For it was Patrick who first introduced Major Hambrough to the suspected murderer, Alfred Monson, and wove him into a complex financial web. Both before and after the trial, Patrick was bankrolling both Major Hambrough and Monson. Where the money was coming from, and how he expected to recoup his losses, is a mystery, but his father probably lived with Patrick until he died at the age of 95 and Patrick was probably responsible for his financial affairs.

Patrick had known Monson, a 32-year-old married bankrupt, for years. Monson (Figure 10.8, Rugby School and Oxford) had an aristocratic bearing and background and plausible credentials. His uncle was the ambassador to

Vienna. Major Hambrough wanted a tutor for his son Cecil Hambrough, and in 1890 Patrick introduced Monson as suitable. Major Hambrough had been in monetary difficulties and had delegated his financial affairs to Patrick. His son was 18, and when he became 21, on 10 August 1893, was apparently set to inherit a substantial banking fortune from his mother's side of the family in New York.

Cecil fell under Monson's spell. Monson lacked money but lived on credit. He rented a substantial country house, hosting dinners for the locals, and then moved on to the next one without paying his bills. After leaving three such properties in Yorkshire, with Cecil in tow, he moved to Ardlamont, a substantial Scottish estate of 12,000 acres (5,000 ha) in Argyll, with his wife and children, engaging a butler and servants.

Major Hambrough decided that when Cecil inherited the fortune Cecil should spend some of it, £20,000, on buying the Ardlamont estate, which was up for sale. He made a provisional arrangement with the Lamonts that Cecil should buy it when he became 21. As a gesture of goodwill and as a deposit, the Hambrough Bank sent the Monsons a cheque for £250, payable on 10 August 1893.

Patrick arranged a contract for Major Hambrough to pay Mrs Monson £5 each week and a lump sum at the end. All sorts of complex financial arrangements were employed. For example, Mrs Monson brought an action against Cecil for £800 for board and lodging due. The suit was undefended, and as a result, the judgement was sold to PLT for £240 in cash. PLT also insured Cecil's life in case he died before the contract expired. Cecil had a medical check and agreed to sign letters obviously not written by himself. As a result, two New York policies on Cecil's life for £10,000 each, made out in the name of Mrs Monson, were arranged on 4 August 1893. The relevant paperwork was to reach Ardlamont on 10 August.

Figure 10.2: Cecil Hambrough, who died on his 21st birthday.

Cecil, though, died that morning. He had gone rabbit shooting with Monson and another man called Sweeney, alias Scott, promoted by Monson as a chance acquaintance who was an engineer of boat engines, but who turned out later to be a bookmaker's clerk from Surrey, a friend of Monson's.

In 2007, we visited the spot where Cecil died by taking the boat to the Cowal peninsula from Tarbert. The remote 640-acre Ardlamont Estate, at present surrounded by woodland and frequented by golden eagles, rebuilt in 1820, is in an idyllic spot, looking down the estuary towards Arran (see Figure 10.4, p. 120).

Cecil died along a track about 300 yards from the house. Monson claimed that he and Sweeney had been about 50 yards ahead of Cecil, when they heard a shot and found him lying on the ground, bleeding from a head wound, having accidentally shot himself. The pellets were from Monson's gun, but Monson claimed that he and Cecil had exchanged guns after they left the house.

Ardlamont's butler had found Monson and Sweeney cleaning their guns. He was told that Cecil had shot himself. Sweeney disappeared, until his arrest warrant had expired. At Monson's subsequent trial, in Edinburgh, in early 1894, it was established that the bullet which killed Cedric was fired from 5 to 15 feet away. Damage to a nearby trees suggested that the bullet had been fired horizontally. The evidence of these experts was not enough to convince the jury.

The trial was a national sensation. In all, 110 'witnesses', including PLT, gave evidence.[7] There were over a hundred reporters at the 10-day trial in Edinburgh, and in *The Scotsman* the report of the trial extended to 173 columns. Monson had an articulate defence counsel, who induced the jury to record the uniquely Scottish verdict of 'not proven'. He made light of the other accusation, that of attempted murder the day before. Monson and Sweeney took Cecil to sea in a rowing boat after inserting a plug in the bottom of the boat. Once at sea, they apparently removed the plug Cecil could hardly swim. The weight of circumstantial evidence was biased towards Monson as the murderer, and yet the jury could not bring themselves to be 100% certain.

Most contemporary accounts suggest that the general public felt that Monson was guilty.[8] Several books have been written about the trial.[9] A television drama about the trial, *Murder Not Proven*, was aired on 17 May 1984, with Allan O'Keefe playing the role of Beresford Patrick Crichton Stuart Loftus Tottenham. Edward Sweeney did not turn up until a long time afterwards. The verdict enraged Cecil's friends. For many years, on the anniversary of his death, notices appeared in national newspapers stating 'Sacred to the memory of Cecil Dudley Hamborough, shot in a wood near Ardlamont, August 10th 1893. "Vengeance is mine, I will repay", saith the Lord.'

Monson walked free, but the cordial relationship between Monson and Patrick broke down. In fact Patrick had more than met his match in the intelligent, unscrupulous and lying Monson.

Somehow, Monson had managed to cash the £250 advance cheque before Cecil died. The bank stopped the cheque and held Patrick responsible for the money. To release the funds, he sold for £165 a considerable amount of furniture and personal effects which he had put in store for the Monsons. Monson successfully sued PLT for £250 for the value of the furniture, and when he could not pay,[10] Patrick was given a prison sentence of three months' hard labour.

Figure 10.3: Alfred Monson.

Figure 10.4: Ardlamont House through the trees. This site had been the headquarters of Clan Lamont from the fourteenth century onwards, and the base for their bloody skirmishes with the Campbells. The 21st Clan chieftain sold it in 1893, a few months before the Monsons moved in.

Once he emerged from prison, Patrick sued Monson for the £250 which the Monsons had appropriated as a deposit for Ardlamont, and for which PLT had been held responsible.[11] When Madame Tussaud's waxworks decided to set up a Chamber of Horrors exhibit of Monson, Patrick sold them a gun and a suit of Monson's for £100. Monson sued Tussaud's for libel, and won his case.[12] Yet he was only awarded the princely sum of a farthing (a quarter of a penny) in a case that contributed to the framing of libel laws all over the world.

A couple of years later, Monson's wife sued him for deserting her and his six children. Monson sued for divorce, citing two co-respondents, including Cecil Hambrough. Given the daily reporting of all these trials in *The Times,* it was not surprising that this 'West End moneylender' Beresford Patrick Creighton Stuart Loftus

Tottenham, as a jailbird and a bankrupt, found it difficult to find clients.

By that stage, hardly any other descendants of his grandfather, Isaac Newton Wigney, were left in London. If the God-fearing descendants of George Adolphus, living in north London at the time and stalwarts of Spurgeon's Tabernacle, had realised that Patrick was really a scion of the Wigneys, they would have been horrified.

11

ISAAC NEWTON WIGNEY'S OTHER CHILDREN

ISAAC NEWTON and Caroline had five children younger than Clarence, some of whom, like Clarence, had rather dramatic lives. When Isaac Newton Wigney died in 1844, Clarence (the oldest), Adelaide, Augusta and Henrietta were all teenagers, and Cecil was only nine. Presumably their financial security was assured because their mother, living with her own mother at Devonshire Place in London, came from such a wealthy background. It was Henrietta and Cecil who ultimately had marriage difficulties.

Three of the girls were married by 1854, all into families associated with the army or the Church. Constance, who died young, Augusta and Adelaide had relatively uneventful marriages. Augusta married John Farrer, and had three sons, and three daughters. Their oldest son, for example, was William Dent Mountjoy Cecil Phillips Farrer, of Gurthalougha of County Tipperary. He was educated at Eton and was a lieutenant in the Grenadier Guards. Another son was in the 8th Hussars. Her daughters were called Hyacinthe, Violet and Irene. Hyacinthe Farrer became the second wife of Alastair George Hay-Drummond, the son of George Hay-Drummond, 12th Earl of Kinnoull.

Figure 11.1: Adelaide, Isaac Newton Wigney's eldest daughter.

Adelaide married Richard Ramus, the son of Colonel Ramus. She only lived for another seven years, and her daughter Adelaide was, by 1901, unmarried, of independent means, and living up north with relatives.

Henrietta, daughter of INW and Caroline, did not marry until 1859, when she was 28. Charles Peyto Shrubb (CPS), the son of the vicar of Boldre, Near Lymington in Hampshire, was six years younger. His sister, Charlotte, had married one of the Ramus family, into which Henrietta's sister Adelaide had already married. Charles was due to inherit the Merriswood Estate, Guildford, which has since become the campus for the University of Surrey.

At first, things went well. The 1861 census records that they were living at 33 Little Vicar's Hill, Boldre, Lymington. In 1871, Charles still lived there, but Henrietta Shrubb was living with two servants at 136 Hampton Wick, Kingston-on-Thames.

The *Evening News* for 13 July 1871 reported that a young lady, Miss Emily Sullivan, 19, had eloped two weeks previously to Cork, Ireland, with a married man called Charles Peyto Shrubb of Lymington. Her father, a local businessman,

> traced the pair from Reading to London, to Bath, and to Cork, where he met Shrubb accidentally yesterday. He seized him, assaulted him, and then gave him up to the police on a charge of abduction and robbery of jewels and money.... Miss O'Sullivan is heiress to a fortune of £45,000, and a ward in Chancery. Shrubb, who spent the night in prison, complained bitterly of the hardship and indignity. He had brought with him a complete service of plate, and was unable to eat his food off the prison platters. The parties returned to England today.[1]

By 1881, Henrietta (Wigney/Shrubb) was living in Bray in Berkshire with her sister Augusta Farrer, whose husband John had died in 1873. By 1891, she had moved in with her brother Cecil in East Moseley, Surrey. Meanwhile, in 1881, Charles was living with his 'wife' Emily Shrubb (29), Charles (b. 1878) and Amelia (b. 1880), and two relatives, Fanny and Jesse Adams.

In March 1896, Henrietta died. Charles Peto Shrubb must have been aware of this, because in the same month, he married Emily at last. Henrietta, however, had the last word after thirty years of separation, for her gravestone defiantly proclaims 'Henrietta, wife of Charles Peto Shrubb'.

Charles died in 1899, but in 1901 Emily C. Shrubb was living at 142 Merriswood Court, Guildford, with two sons Charles and Henry (b. 1882).

Figure 11.2: Henrietta's gravestone.

Cecil Wigney, the youngest of INW's children, married Louisa Carolina Walsh, a considerable heiress, in 1863. At that time he was a captain in the Indian army, at home on sick leave.[2] He was 28 but she was 40. They had known one another since he was a boy, but one wonders if he married for love. When they married she settled two-thirds of her annual income (£1,200) on him for life and this enabled him to retire from the army on half pay.[2] They moved into Bear-hill, Twyford, Berkshire, where Louisa had previously lived with Colonel and Mrs Fuller, her uncle and aunt.

Cecil and Louisa were on good terms for four years, but then Cecil's conduct changed. He was frequently away, refusing to account for his absence, and sometimes violent towards her. He had a roving eye. Differences over money matters mounted when Louisa inherited another £1,000 a year in 1876. Eventually, in 1879, Cecil eloped with a local girl. They had been living together at various places as man and wife when Louisa successfully petitioned for divorce in 1879.[3]

Cecil married his lover Grace Margaret Edwards in Westminster the following year. He was 48 and she was 38, yet they had five children. The three surviving girls died in their late teens, in 1902–03, so close together than one suspects an epidemic, such as tuberculosis.

Cecil and Grace's two boys were horsy. Clement went out to South Africa to work with horses but died there at 28. Clarence Robert D'Arcy Wigney, known by all as 'Major Bob', fought in the First World War and then made a career in horse racing. He was a successful Clerk of the Scales, handicapper and racehorse auctioneer, becoming 'Clerk of the Course' at Folkestone, Plumpton, Pershore, Hawthorn Hill and Cheltenham. The Bob Wigney Handicap is still an annual feature of Cheltenham races. Unfortunately, his only son was *mentally* handicapped and died at the age of thirteen in 1940. So Major Bob was the last of the male descendants of INW, with the Wigney name. There were no Wigneys at his well-attended memorial service at St George's, Hanover Square in April 1959.

So Henrietta and Cecil, at least, had their financial security compromised by the trials and tribulations of marriages on the rocks. Constance had been the first of Isaac Newton's daughters to marry, but thankfully, she died without realising what her son had been up to, which we revealed in Chapter 10.

12

UPSTAIRS DOWNSTAIRS

THE SCHISM of the Wigney clan into two groups, the haves and the have-nots, is partly the result of George Adolphus's decision in 1813 to marry for love rather than for money. William's shrewd business sense, and his luck in being in the right place at the right time, had turned him from a pauper into a rich man. His sons and daughters acquired the social accoutrements of high society, whilst many of his nephew's descendants found it difficult to make a living.

As we have seen, William's direct descendants were well off. Their main purposes in life were to make and maintain the right social connections, act in the way that society expected, and to make themselves even richer. At dame school, school, in the army, and at parties or balls, they established a network of contacts. They grew up in houses with cooks, servants, grooms and gardeners, with easy access to horses and carriages. Many of the men were army officers abroad for a time, and it is tempting to suggest that they were dehumanised by the experience. Although they were nouveau riche rather than landed gentry, they mixed in circles where they had plenty of time and money to indulge themselves and become selfish. By 1963, no Wigney men remained from this branch of the family.

It is a paradox that Isaac Newton Wigney was the person most afflicted by the demise of the Wigney Bank in Brighton, but nevertheless, his family and descendants carried on in London as if nothing had happened. On the other hand, after the Wigney name in Brighton became mud, George Adolphus and his descendants, who had not been involved in the bank scandal at all, were probably most affected by it.

As we shall see, most of George Adolphus's descendants were God-fearing, enterprising, and worked hard with their hands. Like George himself, they had ideas and business acumen, and improvised to make a living. Many were content to aim for continual self-improvement, laced with service to others, instead of leading a selfish, hedonistic existence. Ultimately, this ethic stemmed from the strong religious convictions of George Adolphus's wife, Mary Ann Wilmshurst, and her parents.

Riding high in the most salubrious parts of London and the home counties, at a time when Britain was becoming the richest country in the world by exploiting the colonies and industrialisation, William's direct descendants were insulated from the fluctuating undercurrents of economic change. GA's children and grandchildren, however, encountered the expansion of slum housing and pollution, as the enclosure acts drove farm labourers from the countryside to the towns and new industries were established. Family sizes were still large, and work was scarce. It is not surprising that some became convinced that life might be better in the colonies.

In the 1840s and 1850s, Isaac Newton's family were occupying a grand house in a plush Regency terrace in Central London, leading a social life devoted to finding the right person to marry, with servants, horses and carriages. It is galling to think that at the same time, some of their cousins, nephews and nieces were trying to eke out a living in slums and factories in some of the suburbs. Did they know one another? Did they care?

PART IV

GEORGE ADOLPHUS'S DESCENDANTS

13

GEORGE ADOLPHUS WIGNEY & THE AUSTRALIAN EMIGRATIONS

GEORGE ADOLPHUS'S legacy was written in descendants and genes rather than money. He himself did not die until 1872, at the age of 82. By then he had over 40 great-grandchildren, particularly Wigneys, Virgos and Crumps, but his wife Mary Ann (Wilmshurst, daughter of the God-fearing Evangelical silversmith) had died, and he had remarried a spinster named Anna Maria Constantine. He stayed in central Brighton, being listed as a wine merchant and grocer in New Street in 1851.[1] By then he had sold the remains of his brewery, but he had his legacy from William, and his income from his books, which are still in print. His will is written from 2 Church Street, still a prominent Grade II listed house attached to 23 and 24 New Street, next door to the Unitarian Chapel overlooking the Brighton Pavilion grounds (Figure 6.3).

George Adolphus advised, supported and kept in touch with his children as they grew up and established families of their own. His own early marriage was chaotic., William the Banker had strongly advised against GA's marriage to Mary Ann, and cut off funding. As GA's son Fred later put it, GA was

> fully determined to stand on his own merits and fight the battle of life for himself and become as great a man as his

uncle: but a rough time he had of it, and a family came on apace to retard his progress towards a position of wealth and fame.

We are blessed with several contemporary accounts of what life was like for GA's descendants. GA apparently left his own memoir, but we have never found it. His daughter Martha Mudge (Martha II) left a graphic account of her voyage to Australia with two of her younger brothers, George Adolphus II and William IV, on *The Statesman* in 1852 (see later in this chapter). GA's son Frederick II sailed to Australia in 1858, on *The Shooting Star*, with sister Catherine, and ultimately became a newspaper proprietor. In *The Past and the Present* he describes his early life in Brighton.[2] Best of all, grandson William V emigrated to Canada, with his father and three brothers in 1857. Although he himself never arrived in Canada, opting to remain in America, he left a fascinating autobiography.[3] Fifty years later, he wrote about a return visit to his Wigney relatives in north London.[4] All these scribes contribute unwitting-ly to the following pages.

George Adolphus and Mary Ann Wilmshurst, balancing business lives with ten children in sixteen years, understandably kept a chaotic household. Frederick, their fifth child, records being a rebel from the start.

No sooner that I could walk than ... I was put on my brother's back and taken to dame school: rebellion ensued ... upon one occasion I commenced my war-dance and kicked my way though the parlour window, which sad event, I think, must have settled my fate, so that before I was seven years old myself and a sister and a younger brother were Banished one Siberian-like morning to the Misses Starvems' boarding school, at the little town of Billingshurst, where at the end of six months, we were found so cured of corpulency, and so little likely to survive much longer, that we were removed

home for a time. However ... I soon found myself consigned
to the care of an old soldier, a strict disciplinarian, from whom
I soon deserted, and fled for refuge to my big brother Joe, a
broad-shouldered good-natured young fellow who had
imbibed the same Christianity as my dear mother. Joe and I
were very happy ... and if I became too rebellious Joe would
give me a good cuffing, which I knew was all for my good.
He took me into the sea and ducked me until I was nearly
drowned....

Joe was of course Joseph II, the oldest brother (b.
1815), whom we shall meet later, the ancestor of a
multitude of Wigneys.

Of the other children, Mary Ann (1817–58) was the
only one to stay in Brighton *all* her life. She married
George Virgo, an ironmonger, and spawned a rich crop of
Virgos. Ellen (b. 1820) married William Crump and
produced Crumps, largely in the Isle of Wight. Stephen
(b. 1824) became an accountant and Baptist minister, had
a son and six daughters, but at one stage was convicted of
appropriating mission funds and was sent to prison for
two months. His son Stephen III became a jeweller in
Brighton and was married, but in 1873 appears to have
been committed to a mental institution and is untraceable
afterwards. Emily (b. 1828) had an illegitimate child,
Rhona, before marrying a Mr Staite, moving to Southsea,
and producing three more children.

The economic climate was difficult in the 1840s. Despite
the rush from the countryside to the towns, and Brighton's
success as a holiday resort, good jobs were difficult to find.
GA's sons, especially Joe (Joseph II), were in and out of
work. Frederick himself became a printer, started a business
in New Street (1850), and produced an edition of one of his
father's books[5] before being declared bankrupt in 1856.[6] At
the same time, the colonies beckoned. They offered a new
start in life and opportunity, mentioning the potential for
those willing to take the plunge. Some of those who had

taken the long voyages to America or Australia gave lectures on their return, mentioning the potential to create farms and land ownership. Gold rushes even offered the hope of a quick buck.

Figure 13.1: Mary Ann Virgo.

After such a lecture in Brighton in 1852, Martha II and her husband Daniel Mudge, a carpenter, decided to sail to Australia. GA approved, and donated money. Martha II, her husband and her two youngest unmarried brothers,

William IV (b. 1831) and George Adolphus II (b. 1829), set sail from Portsmouth on *The Statesman* in July 1852. Frederick II joined them on *The Shooting Star* in 1858, with five young children and his second wife.

Figure 13.2: Ellen Crump.

His sister Catherine (b. 1818), who had established herself as a milliner next to her father's wine and grocery store in New Street, also sailed to Australia with Frederick II, where she found a husband (Richard Matthews) and had a son. Since Joe (Joseph II) also emigrated to Canada in 1857 with half his family (Chapter 13) six of GA's ten children emigrated, and George Adolphus never saw them again.

Two strikingly eloquent letters written by Martha to her father appeared in the *Brighton Gazette*[7] at the time. They describe the voyage and what the settlers found when they arrived in Melbourne 86 days after leaving Portsmouth. The fifty Brightonians on board *The Statesman* were part of the biggest mass exodus from Britain to Australia in one year; about 290,000 joined the gold rush.

Brighton Gazette. *Thursday, 30 December 1852*

My dear Father, – It was my intention to make a daily memorandum, but sea-sickness and the excessive closeness below obliging me to remain on deck, prevented my doing as I could have wished. We left Plymouth Sunday afternoon, June 27th, with a strong head wind, which caused the vessel to lay much on one side, and we were tossing about two or three weeks, and altogether in a deplorable condition. The weather was bright, or I know not what we should have done. Brother William was not sick long, George entirely escaped. My husband and self were very bad for a long time.

We could not take our food 'tween decks, but were obliged to sit above, and lie down immediately after taking anything. Gradually, as we approached the line, and the sea became calmer, we lost our sickness; and now, although the motion of the vessel (when great) causes an unpleasant nervous sensation, I do not expect a return. Having been at sea two months, many little incidents I meant to mention have slipped my memory. One I cannot forget though, which is this:-

July 16ᵗʰ There was a cry of "Sail a head." All crowded to the bulwarks of our vessel. As we gained upon the distance that lay between us I shall never forget the intense interest that seemed portrayed in every countenance. All were silent when alongside, while our captain made numerous enquiries (which he roared through a trumpet). The vessel was a Dutch one, named Caroline Hayns from Rotterdam to Batavia. There followed alternate cheering one another; but darkness coming on, a blue light, a few rockets, a tune from our little band, and we were compelled to part. I cannot convey to you how reluctantly, for although it was a meeting of strangers, yet on the ocean there is a feeling of loneliness as if banished from all that is natural and congenial to us, and the sight of a freight of fellow beings in the same position as ourselves is calculated to call forth all the best feelings of human nature.

July 18ᵗʰ (Sunday morning) Passed the Island of Palma, leaving it to the east of us. The mountains are very high. It was calm, and being just sunrise, I opened my window, fearing we should pass before I could dress, but the proximity to land causing a swell, myself and bed were as completely drenched as if precipitated into the sea. But as salt water does not give cold, and we expect all sorts of misfortunes here, I did not trouble much about it, but shall never forget Palma. Next sighted Madeira and Cape DeVerde Islands.

But the most important matter was "crossing the line," which took place Wednesday, August 4ᵗʰ. First, a car, containing Neptune, wife and children, was drawn up the side of the vessel (they were sailors and boys secretly conveyed into it). They proceeded to the cabin, and, in a pompous speech informed the captain that if he wished the winds and waves to be propitious to him, he must allow them to perform a few of their ceremonies on board. He made an appropriate reply, but begged they would be lenient with the novices. They then proceeded round the deck, accompanied by the band, which consisted of William's ophleclide [sic; more correctly ophicleide] *and three more instruments. A sail was ready filled with water at the side of deck, at the edge of which a seat was fixed, and the*

*juniors among the crew were seated and begrimed with a
mixture of pitch, etc; and although a large razor was passed
over their faces, yet they were not hurt; but when finished they
were, one after another turned into the sheet, out of which they
scrambled as soon as they could. The passengers enjoyed the fun;
and about 30 of them (Mr Lackey among the rest) got served
the same. That over, water was thrown about in all directions,
and every one was wet to the skin. Those females who wished to
witness the sport were allowed on the poop, (a privilege in
ordinary allowed only to cabin passengers), but they did not
altogether escape, as a few stray buckets full found their way up
there. The captain watched the sport, as temper is sometimes lost
on these occasions; but it all ended in good humour. The heat at
the time of year we crossed the line was not so great as at a few
degrees north of it, and the heat is not nearly so intense as the
representations we had heard of it. There was a dreadful
closeness and offensive smell between decks when the water was
being given out; but I found lying in the shade on deck very
comfortable and seldom too hot. We had lively evenings, the
band frequently played and while many danced we sat up in the
bulwarks and watched the flying fish, and a kind of a
phosphorent* [sic] *fish that used to sparkle against the side of
the ship. There was a shark drawn up the poop one Sunday
morning. It came floundering along, and leaped down upon our
deck, much to the alarm of many, but the sailors soon put an
end to his capers. They cut it up with long knives and some
parts were cooked, but it tasted very coarse. The next Sunday a
young man, sitting very near me, was playing with some
gunpowder, and displaying his pistol, having a cigar in his
mouth. By some means the powder flask ignited, and it was
quite a providence he did not lose his arm, and we our eyes, but
the wind blew in a contrary direction, and he escaped with
mutilation of his fingers. The captain was very angry, as the rule
is to give up all powder to his care, and it was understood all
had done so; but there are a great many rules not strictly
attended to, this one in particular. All private lamps are
ordered out at ten at night, and all are expected to be quiet. The*

married people generally attend to this, but there are six cabins opposite, with six single men in each of them and they are often leaping about, quarrelling or playing cards half the night. I think in most vessels these are put in steerage, but as there is such a majority of men it could not be otherwise here. Out of more than 300 passengers there are only 40 females, children inclusive. In the intermediate, in the cuddy they are more evenly divided.

September 17th I am just well enough to write a little additional matter. The last three weeks has been very trying. I have been confined to my bed, and am still very weak. Hope revives when I think how soon we may expect to land. The weather the last month has been very trying. Captain Godfrey chooses "Great Circle sailing", as it is called, and runs down south of Kergueland, or Island of Desolation, and it being winter here, the cold has been intense, snowstorms and the wind blowing as I have never heard. The sailors are obliged to have ropes to walk by on deck, and it is quite dangerous for passengers to go above. Some have had bad falls, and one dislocated his shoulder, which was set again with very great difficulty, but none have lost their lives. Many passengers have laid in bed, but keep themselves warm we could not, as the ice was half an inch thick in our cabins. The surgeon allowed one pint of porter per day from the ship's stores, or I do not know what would have become of me...

About ten days ago, we had a tremendous squall. It was at noon; and we were flying before the wind. Suddenly the loud voice of the captain was heard. All was hurry; the sails could not be furled before a storm of snow and wind caused a frightful heaving of the vessel; the topsails were carried away, and minor injuries sustained. The passengers (doctor with the rest) all ran to assist. It was for a short time very alarming. All next night we went under nearly bare poles, and for a few days it was very squally. I was too ill to see the water at the roughest; but I have seen the waters form an almost perpendicular wall on one side. The sight at such times is more awfully grand than I could ever

*have imagined, and one I should rather witness while on land.
Our bed being the short way of the ship is very uncomfortable,
for when the wind is aft the vessel rolls, and our feet rise, then
sink so low that we can scarcely retain our position; indeed some
have not been fortunate to do so. One Saturday night a large
wave struck one side of the bows of the ship; and about ten men
were dropped with the bottom of their beds and bedding on to
their neighbours in the bunks below. There being but one dim
lamp, you can imagine the confusion and fright that ensued.
Fortunately, none were hurt, but the carpenter had a good
Sunday's job. At first there was a great deal of sport in this
front part of the vessel; the sailors would throw down a pig in
the night. The weather was fine and each one brought out a little
stock, which kept up their spirits......*

*Sundays are particularly dull; there are prayers in the
morning in fine weather, but there have been none lately. Our
thoughts and conversation then turn more particularly toward
the little spot called home, rendered doubly dear by the increasing
distance that lies between us.*

*21st September. I can scarcely collect myself to write, that land,
the long looked for land, is seen at last. We are near the coast of
Cape Otway. The wind is not very favourable, but we hope to
take in the pilot by tomorrow. It is 86 days since we left
Portsmouth.*

*22nd September. The wind changed last night. We rounded the
lighthouse at Cape Otway; the pilot is on board, and we shall
soon be in Portland head, I hope. One thing I must not omit.
There has not been one death; there has been one little girl born;
Mr Tankard's sister, Mrs Hardy, is the mother.*

*Give my love to Mrs Sharp and family, also all friends. Glad to
hear of anyone.*

Care of Mr Juniper, ironmonger, Swanston Street, Melbourne.

*PS Necessary for comfort for intermediate passengers:- Filterer,
spirits and port wine, lamp, portable saucepan and kettle, tin
plates, baking dish, bowl etc; flour, biscuits, gingerbread,*

semolina, arrowroot, sago — all these must be in tin cases; for a couple, 4lb raisins, 4lb currants, 6lb sugar, 2lb or 3lb coffee, 1lb tea, small jar of butter, salted over, after crossing the line it will get solid and good; Dutch cheese keeps best; some ham or bacon, nice relish for breakfast, which we were allowed to cook (little tobacco for the cook); jam, onions, baking powders for bread, effervescing drinks, seidlitz powders, few pills, lamp oil and cotton, eggs greased and put in salt, some tins of preserved meat, little suet, Normandy pippins; warm wrappers and clothes; anything is good enough to wear.

Brighton Gazette, *Thursday, 30 December 1852*

Letter received by Mr G.A. Wigney
Collingwood, October 8th 1852

My Dear Father, — Our vessel anchored in the beautiful bay opposite William's Town on 23rd September. William and I left by the first steamer, which brought us up to Melbourne. Oh, the delightful sensation of setting foot on land! We found the Junipers quite well, and spent the evening with them, and they kindly slept us. Next morning they directed us where we might find a lodging. The town is so full that we could not get lodgings in it; but through their recommendations we procured two empty rooms at Collingwood, a distance of about half a mile from the town, and upon a beautiful hill. Our rent is £1 per week, which is far less than two rooms could be got for in Melbourne. My husband and brother George came on shore with the luggage on Saturday, 25th, and on the following Tuesday got situations at a coachmakers — my husband £4 and W. £3 per week. This may seem astonishing, but I must tell you how trade stands here. Everything is enormously dear. Many of the successful gold diggers do not mind what they give for things. Then there has been, and still is, such an influx of emigrants that provisions have risen very high. The passengers from the Statesman, finding things so dear, were obliged many of them to sell clothes and other matters before they could pay to get up to the diggings. Some have done as we are doing, staying and earning, and then going some future day. Those trades people who have been here some time now reap the benefit, as they get cent per cent for their goods; but to a settler it is trying, and many from our ship, when they landed, were quite discouraged; they were obliged to pitch their tents upon the beach, or some distance from the town (as it is against the law within a certain distance). Poor things, it was quite distressing. But meat is cheap, 4d. and 5d. best pieces; and after getting up their strength they are, no doubt, in better spirits. Bread, 2s the 4lb loaf; English cheese, 2s.6d. per lb; colonial 2s.; butter, 2s.6d.; a load of wood, from £2 to £3.10s.; a large cask of water from the river is 2s.6d.; bakings, 6d. weekdays, 1s. Sundays; tea is only 1s.8d, per lb; sugar about the same as in England; cabbages, 1s each, and fruit proportionately dear. Servants in general cannot be got; and washing is from 7s.to10s. per dozen pieces, so that those that wish to get on must work. My husband has the offer of making a number of cradles to sell to the diggers. He will accept the job, and as George is not in anything yet, he will teach him to assist, ... carpenters, bricklayers, brickmakers, paperhangers, bakers, tailors, watchmakers and shoemakers are trades that command good wages, and there are plenty wanted; also any one that can take care of horses, and drive drays. When a man can get forward enough to get a horse and dray he can go and cut wood or fetch water, and his earnings are incredible. If we have our strength and health, I have no doubt we shall do very well. Furniture is very dear. I much regret we could not afford to bring ours; I think it would have sold for three times as much as we gave for it in England... Mr Juniper and John are soon going to the diggings. You hear only of the fortunate diggers; but there are many tradesmen here doing far better than the majority of diggers. So that altogether our party seem most inclined to grasp the substance rather than run the risk of catching at what might prove to be a shadow. Mr Juniper only goes when he can spare time to leave his business for a short time. At present the roads are so muddy that it is £5 10s. per cwt. for luggage from Melbourne to the diggings, and one gets nearly up to the middle, as it is not possible to ride. There are a great number of auction sales. Anyone that has goods to sell takes them to the auction rooms, so that if George had had his type he might have done well at jobbing; as it is we are all living together, and I dare say he will do well under my husband's superintendence. There is certainly more scope for a working man when he has once got a little money. The town is not paved nor lighted, but it is nicely laid out, and has plenty of places of worship in it....Last Sunday we went to a church close by us; and heard a good gospel sermon, preached extempore in a plain manly manner. It put me in mind of Exeter. We all liked it much; but as my time is hastening, I must conclude. Please write soon. I am anxious to hear of Mary, indeed I long to hear of all. My heart yearns to see you, and all my dear friends. I hope to have that privilege again. This country is beautiful; but there is something so inexpressibly painful in the thought that you are so far away. I enclose a note for Uncle Benjamin. The boys unite with my husband and myself in love to Joseph and all the family. Mrs Juniper desires her love and thanks to your wife. We are all picking up, and eat heartily. I intend, if spared, to write again in a month. Write soon, and you will oblige,

Your affectionate daughter, Martha Mudge

Melbourne and the other five main Australian coastal settlement areas certainly presented in the 1850s plenty of the opportunities for personal advancement, just as the West Riding of Yorkshire had a hundred years earlier. The Halifax area, however, had been colonised over the previous two thousand years, a road network and established villages were already in place, and the watery slopes were ideal for cloth manufacture. The Australian settlers had to tame the natural environment from scratch, and many had no particular farming or tradesman skills.

Daniel Mudge, however, was a carpenter. He and Martha quickly settled down and produced a family. The Mudges became established in farming in the Ballerat area of Victoria. One of Martha's granddaughters, Lilian married Ernest Baumgarten, whose father Gustav was acquitted of supplying horses to the Ned Kelly gang. They ultimately ended up in Toowoomba, Queensland. Several descendants still survive, including Reids and Slacks.

George Adolphus II, a printer, resumed his old profession, rapidly taking up the printing of the *Particular Baptist Magazine*. This may have been the reason for his conversion and baptism. By 1859, he was married with four children, and by 1877 he and wife Amelia had had thirteen, though only four survived infancy. He remained mainly in the Ballerat area, although some of his children ended up in New South Wales. Amongst his great-grandchildren are Ian Wigney, who with Katherine Bell has edited and written various psychological texts and guide books, and Brian Wigney, who married Australian Olympic hurdler Gloria Cooke; one of their children is Michael Wigney, a High Court Judge.

William IV, who travelled out with Martha and GAII, became a coachbuilder in Ballerat. He married Harriet Burton, the sister of George Adolphus II's wife and when she died, married again. Amongst his nine children was a well-known nurse, a music teacher, a writer and a couple of tailors. None of his six grandchildren produced any surviving children of their own.

Six years later Frederick II, also a printer, reached Melbourne on *The Shooting Star* in 1858 with his unmarried sister Catherine, the milliner. Both had been living with their father at his premises at 23/24 New Road, near Brighton Pavilion. The 1851 census shows Frederick living there with his second wife (Elizabeth Bax) a servant, Sarah Bax, and his first two children, one of whom was Frederick John (aged three). Five years earlier, Frederick's first wife had died, together with their first son, aged two months. Frederick and Elizabeth had five children by 1858, whom they took to Australia with them.

By the time they arrived Ballerat was beginning to develop rapidly into the 'Athens of Australia' on the basis of the gold rush. Frederick II not only had printing skills but ultimately turned into an imaginative journalist who could write elegant prose, reflecting his father's literary skills. Eventually he became the editor of a Ballerat newspaper and then the proprietor of the *Melbourne Herald*. In 1885 he wrote a memoir, *The Past and the Present*, which contains many valuable recollections of his early life in Brighton. But it took him time to establish himself.

His son Ebenezer died soon after he reached Melbourne. After Elizabeth died too, in 1862. Frederick was inconsolable for a year. He lost his job, spent his time writing poetry day and night, took no care of his children, wandered around the area and eventually was confined to a lunatic asylum for two weeks.[8] During that time it was established that he was without money or property of any kind. He wrote a letter to the *Ballerat Times* explaining what life was had been like in the asylum.

Eventually he recovered and married for a third time, to Anne Croker, and had more children. This gave him the stability he needed to develop a career. He worked on the *Evening Post* in Ballerat, but ultimately became a printer and stationer. Eventually he became a jobbing journalist in Adelaide, and then moved to Melbourne. Amongst his great-great-great-grandchildren from his first marriage there is a well-known South Australian cricketer and an Australian Rules footballer. Their great-great-grandfather, Frederick's son Frederick John, ultimately farmed in Western Australia where his badly

decomposed body was found in a shed in 1896.[9]
Frederick has great grandchildren still living from his
third marriage to Anne Croker.

Frederick's older sister Catherine, who travelled to
Australia at the age of 40, married and had a child. Ian
Mathews is a current descendant.[10]

So the vigorous Wigney community in Australia at
present began when five of George Adolphus' children
joined the mass emigration of 2 per cent of the British
and Irish populations to Australia in the 1850s.

What happened to those who stayed behind to eke out
a living in Britain?

14

THE JOSEPHS & THEIR EVANGELICAL LEGACY IN BRITAIN

OSEPH II (1815–1877), the eldest son of George Adolphus, and his eldest son, Joseph III (1838–1889), made just as great an impact on society as old William Wigney or his nephew George Adolphus, but in a different way. Their long-term legacy to their children and grandchildren was a strong evangelical Christian faith. This sustained them in coping with the slings and arrows of outrageous fortune, and provided hope for the future to counteract despair. It also ensured that they could be supported by a strong social network of like-minded friends and acquaintances when things became tough.

When Joseph II was born in 1815 in Brighton, his father George Adolphus was only 25, trying his brewing experiments, perhaps working part-time in the coalyard, and distracted. As Joe grew up, as Frederick II the Australian printer indicated,[1] he played a major role in caring for the younger siblings of the large and growing family as a parent substitute, especially during Mary's confinements. We assume that GA could not afford servants, and that Joe took his younger siblings to school and went to school himself whenever he could fit it in. Eventually, as his father established his brewery, Joe began to work for him there, Ultimately, with his experience, when his brothers and sisters demanded less of his time, he found a job at a brewery in Pirbright, about 25 miles away.

In Pirbright he met Mary Rose, probably at an evangelical church, for she, like Joe, had been brought up in a family with strong religious convictions. She was five years older than he was. He seems likely to have had a particularly stable marriage, but in Britain at least, he never escaped poverty or job insecurity. He moved to work at a larger brewery in south London, and they rented a house in St George's Road, south of the Thames in Lambeth. There Joseph III, the first of their eight sons, was born in 1838. Joseph III was destined to stay in London all his life, become a gauge maker, and bring up nine children of his own in a strongly evangelical atmosphere. His parents Joseph II and Mary Rose surprisingly had no daughters.[2]

The boys followed in quick succession, so that by the time William V appeared in 1845 he had five elder brothers. He remembers visiting the old ladies in the almshouses with his mother, and she took him to Bedlam nearby, where 'I looked through the iron fence at the peacocks and listened with glee to the poor maniacs as they struggled in their padded cells.' His recollections[3] reflect how tough life was for ordinary people in mid-nineteenth-century London.

William V's older brothers went to a local Anglican parochial school. William himself went to school whenever he could, but it seems likely that most of his effective education took place in his late teens, after he had fought in the American Civil War! His brothers left school early to earn money for the family. For instance when Stephen II, four years older, was ill, William V, aged eight, stood in for him at a local store, working fourteen hours a day for 18 pence a week. Next year, he substituted for

Stephen for several weeks at a boot-maker at Newington, earning the princely sum of 25p a week for a fourteen-hour day. Sundays were the highlight of the week, when Joseph II and his younger brothers walked three miles to the Salem B Baptist chapel and back.

A period of immense uncertainly followed when Joseph II lost his job. The whole family had to move near another brewery in Marylebone. When Joseph II became unemployed again, his father George Adolphus came to the rescue and set Joe up in a little brewery of his own, in Paradise Street in Lambeth. This was never a success. In a few months, the family were in deep distress and poverty. George Adolphus suggested that Joseph II should emigrate to Australia, like his sister Martha, and take his sons with him.

So for a time, Joseph the elder and his sons began to help to fit out a ship destined for Australia. Then Mary Rose successfully pleaded with one of Joe's former employers to take him back. So they smuggled his tools off the ship and Joe went back to work.

For a little while, the family's prospects improved. They moved to 39, Aldred Road, Kennington, London. The two eldest sons, Joseph III and Frederick III, were apprenticed as machinists. Stephen III was employed by a grocer and George Arthur also got a job. But Mary's breathing was becoming more tortured. She had tuberculosis, for which at that time, of course, there was no cure, and Central London in the 1850s was one of the most polluted places on Earth. The family took in help with cooking and cleaning.

In 1855 Mary Rose took to her bed and soon realised that she was about to expire. She called her seven remaining sons to her bedside one by one, expressing her love, blessing them, exhorting them to trust in God, avoid evil and live right. Then she died.

Imagine Joseph II's situation. He had a large bill for funeral expenses, seven boys to care for and then he was thrown out of work again. He engaged a single lady, Ellen Stanion, to look after the boys. He managed to find a brewing job at Plumstead, near Woolwich, then about ten miles out of London. For a while, the boys were content with their lifestyle, although the new housekeeper was unpleasant to them.

Events then moved rapidly. Joseph lost his job yet again. The boys discovered that he had married the horrible housekeeper in secret. George Adolphus suggested that Joseph II and some of his children should go to America, and he would pay for their passage.

But who should go? The two eldest, Joseph III and Frederick III, had four years of their apprenticeship to serve. They decided to rent a room together and live as best they could on the few shillings a week they earned. Stephen III's grocer's job had sound prospects and he could move in with his employer. So Joseph II, wife Ellen and the four youngest boys were bound for America, leaving the three eldest behind. When the packet ship *Northumberland* sailed for New York on 23 April 1857, William V was only twelve years old.

Of those who stayed behind, Joseph III became a gauge maker, and Frederick III an iron turner, at the Royal Ordnance Factory at Enfield. Joseph III (1838–1889) married Amelia Shepherd and they founded a Mission Hall with the Haslar family, who lived at the bottom of the garden of the house which they rented at Waltham Cross. They had nine offspring. One of them, George Wigney III (1871–1917) married Bessie Haslar (1873–1966). They, and their children, were all strongly Evangelical. Bessie continually had the bible in front of her and quoted it.

PHOTOGRAPHERS TO THE QUEEN.

Figure 14.1: Joseph Wigney III, gauge-maker, Waltham Cross,
Heather's great-grandfather.

When Bessie saw the Television Toppers dancing, she
pointed to the screen and declared, 'They are doomed.
They will be confined to hell at the day of judgement.'[4]

She was a strict teetotaller. Had she known of the reliance of the income of the whole family on brewing, she would have been horrified – or perhaps she did find out, because some family documents relating to its brewing past were destroyed at some point.

It is striking that both Joseph III (1838–1889) and his son George III (1871–1917) died early of the same type of stomach cancer, probably caused by ingesting iron dust from the work environment. Frederick III, having worked in the same factory, did not last long either.

It was Stephen III, though, who had the most lasting influence, for he served as Secretary to C.H. Spurgeon[5] for forty years. Spurgeon was the greatest Baptist preacher of the second half of the nineteenth century. After first becoming a pastor at the age of seventeen, he began his Baptist ministry at the New Park Street Chapel in 1858, at the age of 20.

Figure 14.2: George Wigney III, gauge-maker, Waltham Cross, Heather's grandfather.

Figure 14.3: Stephen Wigney, the mainstay of Spurgeon's Tabernacle in London.

congregations of thousands. The Metropolitan Tabernacle at the Elephant and Castle was consecrated in 1861. Spurgeon's 3,800 published sermons run to 62 volumes and he claimed to have read all 30,000 books in his personal library. Stephen Wigney III, who died in 1911, was Spurgeon's right-hand man, editing his sermons, organising his services and tours around Britain, taking bible classes and organising missionaries.[6] The names of his bible class hung over his bed, 'so that they might be prayed for daily and individually'.

In particular, he organised the Colporteurs, those who visited homes selling religious books, often carrying them (porter) round the neck (col). By the time Spurgeon died in 1892, the Colporteurs had made twelve million home visits, but those associated with the tabernacle were in disarray before Stephen Wigney became their Secretary in 1898.

> Shrewd, persistent, sympathetic, and just, he quickly gained the respect of the men under his charge, and within a few years his wise counsels and prayerful interest in the Colporteurs, their families and their spheres of work had gained for him the hearty love of all his helpers [...] The Secretary visited the districts, interviewed many of the local Christian friends who support the work, preached in the Mission Halls and chapels, or presided at public meetings, thus strengthening the hands of Colporteurs and often adding to the funds.[7]

Stephen's son Ernest joined him. One influential Baptist who came under Ernest's spell as a teenager wrote:

> Wigney was a pale-faced, black-whiskered assistant bank manager in Fleet Street, whose frail body housed a flaming spirit. In the late nineties he organised and led the young people of Spurgeon's Tabernacle until they were supporting a dozen missionaries. He drew other churches into the union and set their youth, myself included, to service. He rented an

office on the top floor of the bank building as a centre for his missionary activities, installed a clerk to further them, and refused promotion in his profession so that he could continue to be close at hand.[8]

How the world revolves! Ernest was working in Fleet Street 130 years after his great-great-uncle old William Wigney. The youngest William V (1845–1928), who had emigrated to the United States with his father and stepmother, retained his fervent faith, established in central London in the early 1850s. When he and his wife revisited London from Chicago on their delayed honeymoon in 1907 (!) they stayed with brother Stephen Wigney III, visited a religious gathering at Mundesley in Norfolk with Stephen's son Ernest, and attended all sorts of evangelical services, including some at the Metropolitan Tabernacle.[9]

In the intervening fifty years, William Wigney V had had a dramatic life since he emigrated to America in 1857, at the age of twelve, with his father Joseph II, Joseph's new wife Ellen, and his three brothers. His two lengthy memoirs, summarised in the next chapter, tell the tale.

15

JOSEPH TO AMERICA
& WILLIAM V's AUTOBIOGRAPHY

IN 1857, JOSEPH II and his four youngest sons arrived in New York after a pretty rough five-week voyage. From then on, most of their lives revolved around the Great Lakes region. Akron and Chicago in America and Montreal and Toronto in Canada, were already, in 1857, linked by railways. America, no longer a British colony, was involved in establishing a unified identity. On the other side of the Great Lakes, Canada was British. In contrast to the landscape which Martha and Daniel Mudge met around Melbourne in emigrating to Australia, much of the American and Canadian woodland had already been cleared by settlers and converted to productive agricultural land.

The task was daunting. An unemployed brewer had emigrated to an unfamiliar country, with four sons aged under fourteen and a new wife who did not get on well with them. He had in his favour good health, an optimistic temperament, strong religious convictions, some tools and a few shillings from his father.

After three days they went up the Hudson river by boat, stayed overnight and went up to Akron with their personal effects by horse and cart. In Akron, they found an empty house where they used a large packing case for a table, their trunks and boxes for seats and slept on the floor. Joseph II, the father, decided that he wanted to live in

Canada under the British flag, and so he went to Toronto on his own, where he soon got work. After a few weeks, he sent money from Toronto for Ellen and the four boys to join him. They did, all except William V, who was already working for a local farmer, and at the early age of only twelve, made the momentous decision to stay behind near Akron, Ohio, remaining in touch by mail.

During the next four years William V learnt the skills of a farmer. He was particularly lucky when he worked for Andrew Jackson from the spring of 1858 for three years. Mrs Jackson was kind to him and Mr Jackson was also the village postmaster. There, William had free board, lodging, and clothing, and went to school in the winter.

In 1861 the Civil War had broken out. Seven Confederate states in the south wished to maintain slavery. They decided not to join the northern states, whose President was Abraham Lincoln, in a complete Union. William attended several meetings about the Civil War, and felt the urge to join the army, with several of his acquaintances. So, on 8 August 1862, aged 17, he slipped away to Buffalo to join the 116th New York Volunteers. Although the doctor assured him that he would never withstand the hardships and that he would not live to return, he emerged unscathed three or four years later after seeing some dramatic action.

After a few weeks' training in Baltimore, and a local skirmish, two regiments were towed down to Fortress Munroe to await orders and were crowded onto the same boat for two weeks. There William encountered the first of several illnesses. He caught measles. When he eventually recovered, he was shipped down south with the other invalids to join the rest of his regiment, in a four-week voyage round Florida and up to New Orleans. When he arrived, a case of smallpox was discovered and he and the rest of his regiment were quarantined for three weeks.

At last, he saw some action. After reaching Baton Rouge, he and his regiment became involved in the Battle of Port Hudson Plains, in which Port Hudson was under siege for several weeks before it capitulated.

> For six weeks we lay in the trenches with the Louisiana sun pouring down on us and digging new trenches every night as we gradually moved up. Many died from heat and disease and from lack of water.[1]

Later, William marched for hundreds of miles and took part in many battles as part of the Red River campaign. He describes the sort of conditions he met.

> An old, condemned boat was chartered and two regiments were put on board. There were no berths and we were obliged to lie close together on the floors. We had no way of cooking anything and were obliged to eat hard tack and raw, fat stale pork and drink filthy water.

When they eventually washed their clothes they cleaned out the vermin which were in the seams of their trousers and shirts.

The soldiers also had to improvise. After their victory at the Battle of Pleasant Hill, the regiment's gunboats were stranded up the Red River, having been taken upstream when the water was high. In order to raise the river level and get the boats downstream, the regiment had to dam the river. They had to cut down trees, create cribs, and fill them with stone to block the river, putting flatboats loaded with iron in midstream.

> Then they hitched tugs to these flatboats and opened up the middle of the stream and the gunboats followed each other down through the opening.

After recovering in the Jackson Barracks hospital from a spell of acute diarrhoea, and saving the life of a friend by treating his wounds, William, aged 19, was put in charge of a ward of 50 injured soldiers for several months. Then he requested a return to his regiment. He was given a passage back north, and rejoined his regiment in Virginia, just missing two very severe battles on the way. By then it was the spring of 1865.

> We remained in the valley under Sheridan until the day that President Lincoln was shot, in April, when we were ordered to Washington DC, arriving there to see the train leave with the remains of Lincoln. We were at once given the job of guarding the Old Capital Prison, where the conspirators were confined. We remained there during their trial and execution and were then sent home to Buffalo to be disbanded.
>
> I should not fail to mention the three days celebration in Washington, when each day hundreds of thousands of war veterans, with ragged and dirty uniforms, and many with an empty sleeve, or battle scars, marched in review before General Grant and most of the other victorious generals.

This was of course a particularly bloody war, with over 650,000 killed.

A similarly triumphant celebration awaited William at Buffalo, with a grand banquet at Fort Porter. He sadly admits that

> I had no relatives, or friends to welcome me, and not one solitary person was there to greet me, but all were kind to me and I was happy.

But nearly fifty years later he celebrated more wholeheartedly, when he attended the great gathering of the veterans of the civil war at Gettysburg.

I spent nearly a week, mingling with ex-soldiers, both the Blue and the Grey, and it made a wonderful impression on me to see 5500 men who had fought each other in a most desperate manner for four years, meet in a spirit of true friendship and talk over the struggle when they were enemies.

Aged 20, William was discharged from the army and went back to Akron, where he worked in a grocery store for a year. In the autumn of 1866 he took a momentous holiday in Montreal, visiting his older brother George Arthur, whom he had not seen since they parted company in 1857. While there, probably at a local church, he met a Scots emigrant, Margaret Nimmo. 'It was surely a case of love at first sight.'

William returned to Akron and, lacking the internet, they corresponded by letter. At the end of April William returned to Montreal, and he and Margaret were married on 10 May 1867 in his brother George's house on Princess Street. He was a 21-year-old war veteran and she was 20. The result was a happy union which lasted for nearly 59 years, and produced six children. One of their great grandchildren was Curtis Hessler, who became a Rhodes scholar at Oxford University. William and Margaret renewed their wedding vows in front of 200 friends fifty years later, in the First Baptist Church in Chicago.

Life for William and Margaret was tough at first. Having worked in a Montreal store for a year William lost his job and decided to return to Akron. He and Margaret established a log cabin there. William worked in a cement works and on a couple of farms, and by 1870 they possessed some chickens, a cow and two children, Alice and Willie. But William had to work too hard, and they decided to try city life again. They sold the cow and the chickens, and moved to Chicago in March 1871.

At first, William thought that he was in clover. He only had to work for ten hours a day in a store, and earned nine dollars a week. Then there was the great Chicago fire of 9 October 1871, when much of the city was destroyed. William lost his job. He spent the next few months as a carpenter, before he became caretaker to the 25th Street Baptist Church. His family lived in the basement and his work paid the rent.

Figure 15.1: William Wigney V as a young man in Chicago.

By 1872, say, what had become of Joseph II and the four young sons who emigrated with him? By then William's father Joseph II aged 57, and his second wife Ellen had their own 200 acre farm in Renfrew County, Canada, and Samuel (20) was helping them. George Arthur (29) and Arthur (23) were, like William the youngest, living in Chicago: George Arthur was married and had already produced the third of his six children.[3]

Figure 15.2: Samuel's gravestone in Renfrewshire, Canada. He was only five when he emigrated to Canada. He spent the rest of his life with his father and stepmother, working with them on the family farm.

By 1873 Margaret's mother, from Glasgow, moved in with William and Margaret for seven years.

Samuel died in 1877, aged 25, In 1879 Joseph II wrote to William V to say that he had a bad leg. The next postcard said that Joseph was dead and buried. William rushed north to help Ellen, living on her own and not knowing what to do. Over three weeks, William sold the farm stock and then, despite all the tensions, he regarded it as his Christian duty to take her back to Chicago to live with his family.

He then lost his job when the coalyard he supervised closed. Determined to work for himself, he bought a horse, an old wagon and a licence and began to take orders for coal. This was the start of what became a successful coal business, helped at the start by the earnings of children living with him, Alice the teacher and ultimately, Margaret and Horace.

William and Margaret were even able to buy their own house in 1900. When daughter Margaret (1903), son Horace (1903) and Fred (1910) married and left home William and Margaret were left on their own. Highlights of this phase of their lives were the Chicago World Fair (1893), their honeymoon to Britain for three months in 1907, and their 50th wedding anniversary in 1917.

It was particularly poignant that during their visit based on London in 1907, William and Margaret revisited all their old haunts. These included Pirbright, the house where he was born, the Aldred Road house where William's beloved mother died, Margaret's friends and relatives in Glasgow; London Zoo, Box Hill, Windsor Castle, Kew Gardens.... He even visited his grandfather George Adolphus's old house in Brighton, and met his cousins the Virgos.

The 44-page diary of his visit[2] documents his strong appreciation for the hospitality of brother Stephen III (of the Tabernacle; they had not met since 1857) and all his other nephews and nieces. Yet he was very scathing about a sermon he heard at St Paul's, and many other aspects of London life, compared to Glasgow or Edinburgh.

Figure 15.3: William Wigney V as an old man in the mid-1920s.

While an American is looking for something new and novel, a Londoner thinks that what was good enough for my ancestors 500 years ago is good enough for me. [...] To my mind London appears like a great ocean of bricks and mortar, honeycombed with thousands of dingy narrow passages dignified with the name of streets.... The houses run in crooked rows upon the same pattern and look like regiments of soldiers on parade.... The noise of the traffic is like the thunder of Niagara. The great turbulent mass of trams, buses, trucks, cabs, donkey carts and hand trucks, all rushing about in mad confusion, driven by modern Jehus ... priding themselves on the hairbreadth escapes of the hapless pedestrians who try to dodge between them. The unavoidable policeman ever standing about like stone statues, and one might as well make enquiries of the statue of King William for intelligent information, as to ask a policeman.

William was unimpressed by the Tower of London.

We feasted our eyes on the Crown Jewels which are elegant but which, no doubt, had decorated many a wretched member of royal birth. The whole place seems to be superintended by a lot of Beef Eaters, which look like a lot of overfed old women wearing shapeless costumes with over grown bonnets on their heads.

The British Museum fascinated his wife but not William.

We tried to keep awake and after yawning at the mummies and coveting a snooze in one of the caskets I went out for a walk, leaving Mrs Wigney to her meditations and reflections

William V's older brother George Arthur died long before him. We have met and corresponded with one of his current descendants, Benton Wigney III. Arthur Ebenezer lasted until 1925, leaving four children after a turbulent marriage during which his wife broke a violin over his head when she realised that she was pregnant for a fifth time! Debbie Garcia, one of his current descendants, has contacted us about her family tree.

Figure 15.4: The brothers George Arthur and Arthur Ebenezer, who emigrated to Canada with their father in 1857 and spent the rest of their lives in Canada and the USA. Many of their descendants, surnamed Wigney, still live there.

When William's wife Margaret died in 1926, son Fred and his wife moved in to help William, who died three years later, maintaining the deep religious convictions till the end. We must let him have the last word. As he wrote in 1928,

I am approaching my eighty-third birthday and am in the best of health. My life has been an eventful one and a happy one. I am living in comfort in my own home, without a care on my mind, and calmly awaiting a time when I shall be called to my reward.

16

THE LAST HUNDRED YEARS

T HE VAGARIES of genetics are striking. Joseph the elder and Mary Rose had eight sons. When his father, George Adolphus, died, he had 40 grandchildren. Yet only a handful of males with the Wigney surname remained in Britain, with Bruce Wigney (b. 1946) being one of them. There are plenty of Wigney males, however, in the United States and in Australia. Some British Wigney males only had daughters, or died without leaving children.

The rarity of this surname has made the family tree easy to trace, although we cannot be certain that over the generations other similar surnames have not been altered. Indeed, we have been surprised by the number of surname mistakes made in church records, transcriptions of wills, newspapers and computerised databases.

When William the youngest and his wife visited Britain in 1907 on a delayed honeymoon, he met and stayed with his brother Stephen III and Stephen's son Ernest. Stephen, of course, had stayed in London when William emigrated to America fifty years earlier, and was his only surviving brother in Britain (Joseph III and Fred II had died). Stephen III at the time was Secretary to Spurgeon's Tabernacle. William and Stephen's nephew, George III (son of Joseph III, 1838) married to Bessie Haslar and aged 36, was living in Waltham Cross and working at the Royal Ordnance Small Arms factory at

Enfield. At the time of William's visit, he and Bessie had two sons and a daughter, George Arthur (seven), Bertram (five) and Bessie (three). Later, Wilfrid Charles (1909–2007) was born.

Unfortunately Bessie the younger, by then working as a secretary at the American Express company in London, died in November 1922, aged eighteen. Her death was as a result of endocarditis, following a prolonged attack of influenza. After a seizure, she had been partially paralysed down one side.

Figure 16.1: Bessie Wigney, the younger.

An attractive girl, Bessie had for some time been 'engaged' to Hugh Schonfield,[1] later a prolific author. Schonfield was brought up in a strict Jewish household, but after converting to Christianity, he had become involved with a Christian Missionary group, the 'British Society for the Propagation of the Gospel amongst the Jews' in Waltham New Town in Hertfordshire. He presumably attended the same church as the Wigneys, and worked as a salaried missionary for this society, responsible for conversions to Christianity. Hugh and Bessie were awarded a statuette as the most promising young missionary couple, and Hugh gave Bessie a silver hairbrush set.

Hugh lodged with the Wigney family for some time. He came and went freely, and Wilfrid recalled how Hugh sometimes crawled into his bed to sleep when Wilfrid was in his teens. Apparently Hugh's brother and parents tried to persuade Hugh to move back home, but he would not relent. When Bessie became ill, Hugh moved out, unexpectedly resigning from the Society, although he said that he 'might be able to lead his family to Christ', and did not even attend Bessie's funeral. He later married a wife of Jewish extraction, Helene. After moving out, he always denied his brief period immersed in evangelical Christianity, but there is little doubt that it sowed the seeds of a critical religious imagination. Bessie's mother wrote the Schonfields a heartfelt letter after Bessie died, which is still in the files of the Schonfield Foundation but which they found upsetting and seem unwilling to show us.

Hugh became a respected Jewish scholar, publishing over 40 books, but always retained an attitude of healthy scepticism about the faith into which he had been born. The prime example was the *Passover Plot*,[2] which sold over two million copies and stimulated a well-known film. This put forward the novel concept that Jesus on the cross was drugged temporarily so that his reawakening was meant to give the appearance of resurrection. But it all went wrong.

Wilfrid Charles Wigney, only eight when his father died, eventually became Chief Executive of Ploughley Rural District Council (now Cherwell RDC) based at Bicester, near Oxford. His three children, Heather (b. 1944), Bruce (b. 1946) and Lorna (b. 1952) still live in the Oxford area.

We hope that this account of the history of the Wigney family will prove valuable to future generations.

CONCLUSIONS

A T FIRST SIGHT, Wigneys might seem somewhat ordinary. Closer inspection reveals, though, that they sparkle, reflecting history in dramatic fashion.

In researching and writing this book we were stimulated by Alison Light's book *Common People* (Penguin, 2014). Light, a successful author, managed to reconstruct her family history on the basis of a few newspaper accounts and no family diaries. We have been much luckier because, as we pointed out at the start of this book, not only did several of William's descendants become well-known but many newspapers of the eighteenth and nineteenth centuries document the minutiae of their lives and their court cases, often in fascinating, sometimes excruciating, detail. In addition – again luckily – many left personal memoirs, which have been a wonderful resource and upon which we have drawn freely.

Their stories take place against a background of social change. The Wigneys encounter the decline in the weaving industries, enclosure and the drift from the countryside, the Napoleonic Wars, dramatic expansion of Brighton in the Regency period, frippery and foppery, the Industrial Revolution, economic fluctuations and bank collapses, involvement of rich young men in the British army in India, real poverty, infectious disease, the colonisation of Australia and America, the American Civil War, and the rise of evangelical religion.

We have William Wigney's meteoric rise from north-country pedlar to rich banker and his adoption of the mannerisms and lifestyle of an entirely different social class. He fathers the first MP for Brighton, who marries well. Despite the collapse of the bank, Isaac leaves plenty of well-connected, sometimes roguish, children and grandchildren in London who have servants and private means. At the same time, many of the descendants of George Adolphus, his orphaned nephew, fall on hard times. Several emigrate or fall into menial jobs or unreliable employment, but many are pillars of local society sustained by strong religious convictions.

Furthermore, their fluctuations in fame and fortunes are so well documented. Apart from the usual recourses to local newspapers, censuses and wills, we have nine or ten contemporary accounts which provide detailed information about their day to day lives and ups and downs. Much can be corroborated from other sources; there may well be more revealing documentation to find.

Sagas of family life by authors like Jane Austen, Anthony Trollope and Charles Dickens, and dramas such as *Upstairs Downstairs* and *Downton Abbey*, have gripped the public psyche. But they are only figments of the imagination. The Wigney story is just as dramatic. But it involved real people and real events.

Does this story convey any lessons which we might apply to our own lives? If the area in which you live is in the economic doldrums, be prepared to move somewhere which is thriving or has potential. Be adaptable. It is favourable for a roving male to marry a wife with good local contacts. Now and again every family is capable of producing an exceptional person. Talent and flexibility are more important in life than the best education. Financial success does not ensure happiness. Hard work provides a satisfactory reward.

Above all, have you yourself written a memoir or a diary which may help your descendants to make sense of your life?

NOTES

Chapter 1

[1] The four family trees in this chapter were created by the author.

Chapter 2

[1] Rev. John Waterhouse (1580) *The Story of Wool, Halifax and the Waterhouse Family;* Eileen Power (1939) *The Wool Trade in English Mediaeval History*, Ford Lectures, Oxford: Oxford University Press; Campaign for Wool.
   http://www.themeister.co.uk/hindley/wool.
[2] West Riding weavers: Jenny Uglow (2014) *In These Times. Living in Britain through Napoleon's Wars, 1793–1815*, London: Faber & Faber.
[3] Daniel Defoe (1724–6) *A Tour Through the Whole Island of Great Britain*, London: Dent (1962).
[4] Cloth manufacture in Halifax area:; M. Berg (1985) *The Age of Manufactures, Industry, Innovation and Work in Britain 1700–1820*, Oxford: Basil Blackwell; E. Kerridge (1985) *Textile Manufactures in Early Modern England*, Manchester: Manchester University Press; B.R. Mitchell (1988) *British Historical Statistics*, Cambridge: Cambridge University Press; D.W. Lloyd (1998) *The Making of English Towns*, London: Gollancz (Cassell); D.G. Bayliss (1985) 'Sowerby Bridge 1750–1800: The Rise of Industry', *Transactions of the Halifax Antiquarian Society*, 57–75.
[5] Old William Wigney: birth certificate.
[6] Jean de la Vigne: Ancestry Message Boards: French nobility.
[7] Samuel Smiles (1868) *The Huguenots: Their Settlements, Churches and Industries in England and Ireland* (Harper, New York.

[8] Migration from Ireland: Samuel Smiles (1867) *The Huguenots: Their Settlements, Churches and Industries in England and Ireland*, London: John Murray, ch. 5, p. 126.

[9] Mary Wigney: Church of the Latterday Saints website.

[10] Mr Bruce Wigney, from Oxford, UK, great x 5 grandson to William Wigney's father, underwent a Y chromosome genetic analysis (Y. Family tree DNA. User ID ZTGUGG). The parts of the Y chromosome sequenced are passed unchanged from male to male down the generations. Of the five identical matches, four were in Germany and the other in Poland, all between latitude 51–54° and longitude 7–15°. This corresponds to a study published in *Nature* (see n. 10).

[11] S. Leslie *et al.* (2015) 'The Fine-scale Genetic Structure of the British Population', *Nature* 519: 309–14. Leslie *et al.* divided long-term British residents into 13 distinct genetic tribes. The DNA was sequenced from over 2000 British residents who had all four grandparents living within 50 km of one another. One of the 'tribes' was distinct to the West Riding of Yorkshire. Their closest match was to a group of Germans. These Y chromosomes, of course, go back tens or hundreds of generations. We need to contact these continental 'relatives' to determine if they too have any links to weavers in the Low Countries.

[12] Kirkham Wigneys: William christened, 20 June 1561. Father's name Robert Wigney. National Archives, England Births & Christenings, 1538–1975. https://familysearch.org/pal:/MM9.11/JM29-FSY), citing Kirkham, Lancashire, England.

[13] Wigney surnames: www.ancestry.co.uk; www.FamilySearch.org; Lancashire Parish Registers 1538–1910.

[14] Denton Ings (= Washer Lane). James Wigney II. *Leeds Intelligencer*, 18 and 25 September 1781.

[15] Broadgates copyhold sale: *Leeds Intelligencer*, 25 September 1781; Thomas Wigney II. *Leeds Intelligencer*, 1784, 15 June 1794; 05 October 1794. Freehold estate Thomas Wigney II.

Leeds Intelligencer, 5 October 1795; Leeds Acquirer 12 October 1795.

[16] Sowerby Bridge Fulling Mill: sold John Wigney, Timothy Bates. *Leeds Intelligencer*, 28 February 1775.

[17] Wigney Ing. *Historical Gazeteer of England's Place Names*. Sowerby Bridge. Chapelry of Halifax Chapelry. Modern Field Names. A.H. Smith (1961) *The Place Names of the West Riding of Yorkshire*, Part 3 (EPNS 32), Cambridge. Location obvious from sale advertisement for the Willow Hall Estate, *Leeds Mercury* 10 February 1816, parcels 16–18.

[18] Hearth Tax: 1672 British Record Society (Index Series 121) Hearth Tax Series Volume V. *Yorkshire West Riding Hearth Tax Lady Day 1672*.

[19] Henry and other Soyland Ryleys: In 1667 Henry Ryley, clothier, married Mary Lancashire, from Soyland, in Halifax. An Abram Ryley was born at Soyland in 1671, and two daughters, Martha and Mary, born there in 1690 and 1694. The Wakefield Manor Book for 1709 records a John Ryley with a house and land enclosed off Soyland moor, the insolvent debtors in Halifax gaol 1712–96 include John Ryley, Barkisland, clothier. A James Ryley is recorded at Kirklees, Soyland in 1723. Henry Ryley. *Paver's Marriage Licences, 1667*. (http://www.mocavo.com/Yorkshire-Archaeological-Society-Paver-Marriage-Licences-1660-1664-Volume-2/391911/123). Abram Ryley. *Our Family Genealogy Pages. Mrs Ryley*. Born c. 1664, Abram (b. 1671, m. 1689, Soyland, son, Henry and Mary?). Two daughters Martha, Mary, born Soyland, 1690, 1694. James Ryley. Kirklees, Soyland (1723). John Crabtree (1836) *A Concise History of the Parish and Vicarage of Halifax, in the County of York*.

[20] Gilbert Ryley. 1366. In John Watson (1775) *The History and Antiquities of the Parish of Halifax*.

[21] James Wigney misdemeanours Ancestry, UK Yorkshire, England, Quarter Sessions Records, 1637–1914, orders 1712–20, 1725–29, 1728–33, Indictment 1747–53)

[22] John Wigney marriage: 1751. Records of St John the Baptist, Halifax.

[23] John court case: 1771. Consistory Court; Defamation; sexual slander; no sentence. Cause papers in the Diocesan Courts of the Archbishopric of York, 1300–1858.

[24] Three closes for sale Thomas II. *Leeds Intelligencer*, 15 June 1784. Thomas II death. Broadgates. 7 June 1804. Will proved by Thomas Pollitt, National Archives, 7 June 1804. Cloth dresser. Less than £300. Includes wife Lydia and Sarah Pollitt. National Archives online document IR 26/426.

[25] *Leeds Intelligencer*, 28 February 1775.

[26] Local Homesteads. Kendall, H.P. (1925) 'Some Old Skircoat Homesteads', *Transactions of the Huddersfield Antiquarian Society*, 1–60.

[27] Shaw Hill. Martha Wigney. *Leeds Intelligencer*, 14 May, 180.

[28] Local education: C. Woods (1998) 'Growth of Education in Sowerby and Sowerby Bridge from the Sixteenth Century to the Mid-nineteenth Century', *Transactions of the Halifax Antiquarian Society* NS6, 13–29.

Chapter 3

[1] Bates and Pollitt: *A Brief History of Christ Church, Sowerby Bridge* (2004) and *Grace's Guide to British Industrial History*.

[2] Tabitha: Marriage Certificate. Ancestry UK. 19 February 1775. Mentions John as a cloth draper in Warley.

[3] Elizabeth Wigney marriage. England Marriages 1538–1973. National Archive.

[4] Alice Wigney marriage. *Leeds Intelligencer*, 17 April 1820.

[5] Cronhelms. *Martin Bull's Calderdale Companion* (web) & *Yorkshire Chess History* etc. S.J. Mann (2012) http://www.sjmann.supanet.com/People/Cronhelm,%20Frewde rick%20William.htm

[6] George Hotel, Huddersfield. E. Law (2004) *Huddersfield & District History. History of the George Hotel, Huddersfield, to*

1900.
http://homepage.eircom.net/~lawedd/GEORGEHOTEL.htm
[7] William Wigney obituary: *Huddersfield Chronicle,* 22 June 1861.
[8] Ibid.
[9] Paintings. *Huddersfield Journal* (1844) J.T. Wigney.
[10] E. Law (2003) *History of the George Hotel, Huddersfield to 1900.* Web.

Chapter 4

[1] Defoe quotation: Daniel Defoe (1962) *A Tour through the Whole Island of Great Britain.* London: Dent.
[2] Wilberforce, S. and R. (1838) *The Life of William Wilberforce.* Volume 4. p. 208.
[3] Perspectives on Brighton history and 'attached like wings': Sue Berry (1995) *Georgian Brighton.* Chichester: Phillimore.
[4] Anon (1766) *Gentleman's Magazine* 36, 59–60.
[5] Linen drapery. *Universal British Directory* 1791. Brighthelmstone, pp. 369–76.
[6] Effects of war: Jenny Uglow (2014) *In These Times: Living in Britain through Napoleon's Wars, 1793–1815.* London: Faber & Faber.
[7] Marriage certificate: 23 July 1782, National Archives, XA 30/3, p. 62.
[8] Packhorse: Wikipedia; J. F. Edwards (1987) *The Transport System of Medieval England and Wales – A Geographical Synthesis.* PhD thesis, University of Salford.
[9] William in London (1783) Land Tax Records. Vintry, City of London.
[10] Rickman banking: E. Cobby (1799) *Brighthelmstone Directory.* Lee, Brighthelmstone, Lewes & London.
[11] Blake at Felpham: *Spectator,* 6 May 1916.
[12] Smuggling: Mary Waugh (1885) *Smuggling in Kent & Sussex, 1700–1840.* Countryside Books, Newbury, Berks; Christopher McCooey (2012) *Smuggling on the South Coast.*

Stroud: Amberley Publishing; signage on two Brighton public houses.

[13] Brighton population: Sue Berry (1995) *Georgian Brighton*. Chichester: Phillimore.

[14] Stables: *Hampshire Chronicle*, 28 September 1801; also mentioned National Archives 1818 in relation to a candle factory nearby. See also Sue Berry (1995) *Georgian Brighton*. Chichester: Phillimore.

[15] Killick legacy: Robert Killick, gentleman. Will of 20 April 1796. East Sussex Record Office, 13 December 1800. PBT1/1/68/534 XA26/72/95. See also Universal British Directory 1791. Brighthemstone, pp. 369–76.

[16] Brighton breweries: P. Holtham (2008) 'The Breweries of the Brighton Area', *Sussex Industrial History,* 38, 2–8.

[17] Hanningtons. Local directories and *Views and Reviews. Special Edition. Brighton & Hove.* W.T. Pike & Co., Grand Parade, Brighton.

[18] Family Pew. Assignment of Pew for £40. East Sussex Records Office. 6 June 1801. AMS 5500/1.

[19] Frederick to Bengal infantry 1808. British Library IOR/L/MIL/9/107-269.

[20]. Charles Fleet (1883) *Glimpses of our Ancestors in Sussex* (2nd series) Lewes: Farncombe.

[21] Character. Charles Fleet (1883) *Glimpses of our Ancestors in Sussex* (2nd series) Lewes: Farncombe.

[22] George in Barcombe. Barcombe & Hamsay website. http://www.bandhpast.co.uk

[23] J. R. Hill (ed.) (2002) *The Oxford illustrated History of the Royal Navy.* Oxford: Oxford University Press.

[24] *Morning Chronicle*, 30 June 1845.

[25] Brighton banking: R. Collis (2010) *The New Encyclopedia of Brighton.* Brighton & Hove Libraries.

[26] Iron Duke plaque. Blue plaque no. 12720 in Hove.

[27] Hove and Brunswick Square. Anthony Dale (1967) *Fashionable Brighton 1820–1860.* 2nd edn. Oriel Press.

[28] Will: 25 June 1836. Proved 1 December 1836, London. National Archives PROB 11/1870/444.
[29] Ann's death: 07/08/1859. *Sussex Advertiser*, Tuesday, 16 August 1859.

Chapter 5

[1] Birth certificate.
[2] Grece comment: email Jennifer Smith to Timothy King 12 August 2015.
[3] Constable's diaries: Claire Constable (2001) *The Constables of Horley Mill*. Surrey Mills Publishing Ltd. ISBN 09540359-0-9, and subsequent emails from Jennifer Smith with diary extracts.
[4] Whichelo: J.G. Bishop (1892) *A Peep into the Past: Brighton in the Olden Time, with Glances at the Present. The Inns of Brighton in 1800 and their Associates*. Brighton: J.G. Bishop.
[5] Hanningtons: R. Collis (2010) *The New Encyclopedia of Brighton*. Brighton & Hove Libraries.
[6] Constable associates. Jennifer Smith (2000) 'Reform in the Air', *Sussex Family Historian* 14 (3): 114; Scutt/Cabell relationship. Susan Djabri (1994) 'A Letter from Brighton 1841', *Sussex Family Historian* 11 (3): 92–100.
[7] Rickman poetry: Subscribers to *Poetical Scraps* (1803) by Thomas Clio Rickman of Upper Marylebone Street.
[8] Daniel Constable photography: Biography in Historic Camera, History Librarium, on the web; *History of Photography* (1991) 15 (3): 236–39.
[9] Freemason. United Grand Lodge of England Membership. Lodge of Harmony. 7 August 1824. Brighton: Gent.
[10] Lodging House Keeper: *Pigot's Directory of Sussex* 1832–3.
[11] Brighton esquires: *Morning Chronicle* (London) 2 October 1832, from 'Aristocracy at Brighton', *Brighton Herald*, 27 September 1832.
[12] Vestry Committee: *Brighton Gazette*, 4 April 1825.
[13] Chair Vestry Committee: *Brighton Gazette*, 7 January 1830.

[14] Gas and Coke Committee: *Brighton Gazette*, 3 February 1825.

[15] Chair Gas. *Brighton Gazette*, 12 October 1826.

[16] Brighton Royal British School Society: *Western Times*, 18 October 1828.

[17] Lancashire: *Brighton Gazette*, 4 May 1826.

[18] Oriental Gardens. Brighton Gazette, 15 November 1827.

[19] Chain Pier: *Brighton Gazette*, 17 October 1833.

[20] Fever wards: *Sussex Advertiser*, 11 February 1828.

[21] Slavery: *Brighton Gazette*, 10 December 1829.

[22] Slavery Committee: *Exeter & Plymouth Gazette*, 26 December 1829.

[23] Reform Bill meeting: *Brighton Gazette*, 2 May 1831.

[24] House of Lords petition: *Brighton Gazette*, 29 September 1831.

[25] Dinner: *Morning Chronicle* (London) 13 September 1833.

[26] Death: *Gentleman's Magazine*.

[27] Will (7 March 1829, proved 3 June 1834). Ancestry UK. England & Wales. Prerogative Court of Canterbury Wills 1384–1858.

Chapter 6

[1] Joseph in 3rd Dragoon Guards Canada, British Regimental Registers of Service, 26 June 1779; also marriage certificate.

[2] Joseph marriage certificate: 16 September 1782, Manchester. Ancestry.co.uk.

[3] Joseph in Aldgate, 1791: ancestry.com. London, England, Land Tax records 1692-1932. MS11316/276.

[4] Joseph bankruptcy: *Reading Mercury*, 15 July 1793.

[5] Frederick baptism record with William Wigney's recommendation for Frederick to join the Bengal infantry, 30 December 1808. British Library. IOR/L/MIL/9 107–269.

[6] Joseph death: *Saunders's News-Letter*, Monday, 10 August 1795.

[7] Frederick Wigney (1822–1896), *The Past and the Present,* MS.

[8] GA bankruptcy: *Exeter Flying Post*, January 1818.

[9] Brighton breweries: P. Holtham (2008) 'The Brewers of the Brighton Area', *Sussex Industrial History*, 38: 2–8.

[10] Brewing book: G.A. Wigney (1823) *A Philosophical Treatise on Malting and Brewing.* First edition. G. Verrall, Worthing Press.

[11] GA's place in brewing history: J. Sumner (2015) *Brewing Science, Technology & Print 1700–1880*. London: Routledge.

[12] Bid for share of mother's will. *Wigney v. Chapman.* 1828. Court of Chancery: Six clerks office: Pleadings 1801–42 C 13/1491/78.

[13] Brewery for sale (Richmond Buildings): *Sussex Advertiser*, 1831; sale on 4 February 1831.

[14] GA's will: Written, 24 January 1871; proved, Lewes, 19 September 1872.

Chapter 7

[1] William Wigney's will: 25 June 1836; proved 1 December 1836, London. National Archives PROB 11/1870.

[2] Frederick's baptism: November 1793, St Mary's Newington (b.04-09-93).

[3] Frederick's passage to India: British Library IOR/L/MIL/9 107–269.

[4] East India Company perspectives: Jenny Uglow (2014) *In These Times. Living in Britain through Napoleon's Wars, 1793–1815*. London: Faber & Faber.

[5] Attitudes to Indian wives, and the 'fishing fleet'. William Dalrymple (2002) *White Mughals. Love and Betrayal in Eighteenth-Century India*, London: HarperCollins, and Anne De Courcy (2012) *The Fishing Fleet. Husband-Hunting in the Raj*. London: Weidenfeld & Nicholson.

[6] Indian birth, baptismal and marriage records: East Indian section of British Library, London, e.g. Anne Eliza

(N/1/10f.610), Jane Eliza (N/1/12f.401), Rose (N/1/32f.105), Caroline/Charlotte (N/1/32f.105, India Deaths & Burials B39363-9,India-Easy, GS film no. 512367), Gentloom Aviet (N/1/39f.51), born 9 May 1837, Georgiana Aviet born 17 April 1936.

[7] Frederick medical records: National Archives. India Office Records. IOR/L/MIL/9/259/62v-63 & IOR/L/MIL/9/118/35-36.

[8] Pembroke House and Ealing Lunatic Asylum. British Library: *Asian and African Studies* IOR/K/2.

Chapter 8

[1] Walter family and *The Times*: Dictionary of National Biography.

[2] INW Brighton responsibilities: Anthony Dale (1976) *Brighton Town and Brighton People*. Chichester: Phillimore.

[3] Trial: P.R. Jenkins (2004) *Country Bank Failures. The Brighthelmston Bank*, Pulborough: Dragonwheel Books.

[4] Queen deposit: *Worcester Journal*, 14 April 1842.

[5] Trial: Jenkins (2004), op. cit..

[6] Comments on trial: Charles Fleet (1883) *Glimpses of our Ancestors in Sussex* (2nd series) Lewes: Farncombe.

[7] De Ros: Henry Fitzgerald-de Ros, 22nd Baron de Ros. Wikipedia.

[8] Details of Trial Reports in the *Brighton Herald*, starting on 12 March 1842 and verbatim reports in subsequent editions in particular, 17 June 1842. Similar daily reports in *The Times*.

[9] George contributes 1840: East Sussex Records Office. Release and Covenant (17 April 1841) SAS/N 775; Mortgage SAS-N/778 (19–20 April 1841) and other leases, releases and mortgages at the National Archives under Wigney.

[10] Parcels to London: *Sussex Advertiser*, 10 May 1842.

[11] A. Dale (1967) *Fashionable Brighton 1820–1860*, 2nd edn, Oriel Press.

[12] George's will: 1847. Brewer. National Archives. PROB 11/2060.

[13] Brewery sale: *Sussex Advertiser*, 27 March 1849.

[14] East Sussex Records Office. Brewery buildings in Middle Street and Ship Street, Brighton, purchased by Vallance and Catt in 1850. ACC 3402/1/2/2. Archive of Fitzhugh Gates of Brighton, Solicitors.

[15] William's real worth: analysed in *Brighton Herald*, 12 March 1842.

Chapter 9

[1] Presented at court: *Gentleman's Magazine*, early 1848.

[2] Eton: Index to the Eton School Lists, 1841–50.

[3] *The Times,* 4 January 1849; *Sussex Advertiser*, 9 January 1849.

[4] Hoghton's case for damages: *The Times,* 4 January 1849.

[5] *The Times*, 4 January 1849.

Chapter 10

[1] Constance's marriage certificate: Ancestry.co.uk

[2] PLT's birth certificate: Ancestry.co.uk

[3] Drawing of PLT: *Edinburgh Evening News,* Friday, 15 December 1893.

[4] Financial dealings and bankruptcies: numerous accounts in *The Times*, e.g. 20 and 30 December 1898, 20 January 1899, 10 February 1899, 16 January 1901, 5 August 1905, 19 August 1915.

[5] PLT prevents Rutter from throwing wife over stairs: *The Times*, 25 July 1900.

[6] Emily Banester: birth, marriage and death certificates. Ancestry.co.uk

[7] Murder trial transcript including Patrick's evidence: J.W. More (ed.) (1908) *Trial of A. J. Monson.* Glasgow and Edinburgh: William Hodge & Co.

[8] Contemporary accounts of the murder trial: *The Times*, 13–23 December 1883.

[9] Accounts of the murder and the events surrounding it: W.N. Roughhead (1951) *Classic Crimes*. London: Cassell, pp. 301–68; Jack House (1989) *Murder Not Proven?* Harmondsworth: Penguin, pp. 91–101; Jonathan Sutherland (2002) *Unsolved Victorian Murders*, Derby: Breedon, pp. 176–89.

[10] Monson sues PLT for £250: *The Times*, 12 and 14 April 1894.

[11] PLT sues Monson: *The Times*, 17 May 1895, 15 June 1895.

[12] Monson v. Madame Tussaud's: 30 January 1895.

Chapter 11

[1] *Evening News*, 13 July 1871.

[2] Cecil's Indian Service: British Library. India Office Records. Bombay Army Records. IOR/L/MIL/12/80/233 & IOR/L/MIL/9/222/652-56.

[2] Cecil's marriage settlement: includes a conveyance of rent estates in Jamaica from Louisa Walsh. Berkshire Record Office.

[3] Cecil's divorce: National Archives, Court for Divorce and Matrimonial Causes, 1879 Divorce Court file: 6582. J 77/234/6582. Louisa's divorce. *The Times*, 3 July 1880. Louisa's fortune settlement Probate Division (1882) Volume VII, *Wigney v. Wigney*, pp. 177–87, 15 March 1882 and pp. 228–32, 6 June 1882.

Chapter 12

There are no notes in this chapter.

Chapter 13

[1] George Adolphus and children: addresses and professions listed in Brighton Street directories e.g. *Pigot's New*

Commercial Directory (1828–9); T.A. Swysland and J. Gill (1832) *Directory of Brighton*; *Brighton Censuses* of 1841, 1851, 1861.

[2] Frederick Wigney (1885) *The Past and the Present*. MS. Chapter in his book: Frederick Wigney (1885) *The Crisis of 1885 in South Australia: Its Cause, Effect and Remedy*. Frederick Wigney. Printer, publisher and journalist. Currie Street, Adelaide.

[3] William Wigney (1923) *The Story of My Life*. MS.

[4] William Wigney (1907) *Account of Visit to London*. MS.

[5] GA's book published by Frederick: G.A. Wigney (1850) *An Introductory Treatise on the Theory and Practice of Malting and Brewing*. Brighton: Frederick Wigney.

[6] Frederick's bankruptcy: *Berkshire Chronicle*, 22 August 1856.

[7] Martha Mudge: *Brighton Gazette*, 30 December (1852) and Joyce Collins (2008) *Typescript of Letters from Australia from Brighton Emigrants 1849–1855*. LIA 23,

[8] Frederick's lunacy remonstrance: *Mount Alexander Mail*, Victoria, 7 September 1863; Mr Wigney's remonstrance. *Mount Alexander Mail*, Victoria. 8 September 1863; Treatment of Lunatics. *Mount Alexander Mail*, Victoria, 15 September 1863.

[9] Frederick II's death: At Meenar, Yilgara Railway. *Inquirer & Commercial News*, Perth, WA, Friday, 29 April 1898, p. 13.

[10] Australian descendants: Letters from Karen Wigney, 20 October 2009 and 10 August 2014, and Marilyn Curl 24 April 2013.

Chapter 14

[1] Frederick Wigney (1885) *The Past and the Present*. MS.

[2] Joseph III and his family (London) Census 1841 – St George Southwark (St George the Martyr); Census 1851 –St Marylebone (Christchurch).

[3] William's autobiography. William Wigney (1923) *The Story of My Life*. MS.

[4] Television Toppers. Heard by Heather (1959).

[5] Stephen Wigney: Obituary.

[6] Ibid.

[7] Ibid.

[8] Ernest Wigney: Obituary.

[9] William's London visit: William Wigney (1907) *Account of His Visit to London*. MS 44 pp.

Chapter 15

[1] William's autobiography: William Wigney (1923) *The Story of My Life*. MS.

[2] London visit: William Wigney (1907) *Account of His Visit to London*. MS 44 pp.

[3] Arthur's marriage and descendants: Debbie Garcia (California) email to Heather King (26 March 2007).

Chapter 16

[1] S. Engelking (2015) *A Life for Mankind. The Biography of Hugh Joseph Schonfield*. Create Space Independent Publishing Platform.

[2] Hugh Joseph Schonfield (1965) *The Passover Plot: A New Interpretation of the Life and Death of Jesus* (snippets view) (1996 reprint edn). Shaftesbury: Element.

BIBLIOGRAPHY

A Publications

Bayliss, D.G. (1985) 'Sowerby Bridge 1750–1800: The Rise of Industry', *Transactions of the Halifax Antiquarian Society*, 57–75.

Berg, M. (1985) *The Age of Manufactures, Industry, Innovation and Work in Britain 1700–1820*, Oxford: Basil Blackwell.

Berry, Sue (1995) *Georgian Brighton*. Chichester: Phillimore.

Bishop, J.G. (1892) *A Peep into the Past: Brighton in the Olden Time, with Glances at the Present. The Inns of Brighton in 1800 and their Associates*. Brighton: J.G. Bishop.

Christ Church, Sowerby Bridge (2004) *A Brief History of Christ Church, Sowerby Bridge* (leaflet).

Cobby, E. (1799) *Brighthelmstone Directory*. Lee, Brighthelmstone, Lewes & London.

Collis, R. (2010) *The New Encyclopedia of Brighton*. Brighton & Hove Libraries.

Constable, Claire (2001) *The Constables of Horley Mill*. Surrey Mills Publishing Ltd.

Crabtree, John (1836) *A Concise History of the Parish and Vicarage of Halifax, in the County of York*.

Dale, A. (1967) *Fashionable Brighton 1820–1860*, 2nd edn, Oriel Press.

Dale, Anthony (1976) *Brighton Town and Brighton People*. Chichester: Phillimore.

Dalrymple, William (2002) *White Mughals. Love and Betrayal in Eighteenth-Century India*, London: HarperCollins

De Courcy, Anne (2012) *The Fishing Fleet. Husband-Hunting in the Raj*. London: Weidenfeld & Nicholson.

Defoe, Daniel (1724–6) *A Tour through the Whole Island of Great Britain*, London: Dent (1962).

Djabri, Susan (1994) 'A Letter from Brighton 1841', *Sussex Family Historian* 11 (3): 92–100.

Engelking, S. (2015) *A Life for Mankind. The Biography of Hugh Joseph Schonfield.* Create Space Independent Publishing Platform.

Erridge, John Ackeron (1862) *History of Brighthelmstone.*

Fleet, Charles (1883) *Glimpses of our Ancestors in Sussex* (2nd series) Lewes: Farncombe.

Heaton, H. (1920) *The Yorkshire Woollen & Worsted Industries*, Oxford: Oxford University Press

Historical Gazeteer of England's Place Names.

Holtham, P. (2008) 'The Breweries of the Brighton Area', *Sussex Industrial History, 38*, 2–8.

House, Jack (1989) *Murder Not Proven?* Harmondsworth: Penguin,

Jenkins, P.R. (2004) *Country Bank Failures. The Brighthelmston Bank*, Pulborough: Dragonwheel Books.

Kendall, H.P. (1925) 'Some Old Skircoat Homesteads', *Transactions of the Huddersfield Antiquarian Society*, 1–60.

Kerridge, E. (1985) *Textile Manufactures in Early Modern England,* Manchester: Manchester University Press.

Law, E. (2004*) Huddersfield & District History. History of the George Hotel, Huddersfield, to 1900.*

Leslie, S. *et al.* (2015) 'The Fine-scale Genetic Structure of the British Population', *Nature* 519: 309–14.

Lloyd, D.W. (1998) *The Making of English Towns*, London: Gollancz (Cassell).

McCooey, Christopher (2012) *Smuggling on the South Coast.* Stroud: Amberley Publishing

Mitchell, B.R. (1988) *British Historical Statistics*, Cambridge: Cambridge University Press.

More, J.W. (ed.) (1908) *Trial of A. J. Monson.* Glasgow and Edinburgh: William Hodge & Co.

Pigot's New Commercial Directory (various years).

Roughhead, W.N. (1951) *Classic Crimes.* London: Cassell.

Schonfield, Hugh Joseph (1965) *The Passover Plot: A New Interpretation of the Life and Death of Jesus* (1996 reprint edn). Shaftesbury: Element.

Smiles, Samuel (1867) *The Huguenots: Their Settlements, Churches and Industries in England and Ireland*, London: John Murray.

Smith, A.H. (1961) *The Place Names of the West Riding of Yorkshire*, Part 3 (EPNS 32), Cambridge.

Smith, Jennifer (2000) 'Reform in the Air', *Sussex Family Historian* 14 (3): 114;

Sumner, J. (2015) *Brewing Science, Technology & Print 1700–1880.* London: Routledge.

Sutherland, Jonathan (2002) *Unsolved Victorian Murders*, Derby: Breedon

Swysland, T.A. and J. Gill (1832) *Directory of Brighton*; *Brighton Censuses* of 1841, 1851, 1861.

The Times: *Dictionary of National Biography*.

Uglow, Jenny (2014) *In These Times: Living in Britain through Napoleon's Wars, 1793–1815*, London: Faber & Faber.

Universal British Directory 1791.

Watson, John (1775) *The History and Antiquities of the Parish of Halifax.*

Waugh, Mary (1885) *Smuggling in Kent & Sussex, 1700–1840.* Countryside Books, Newbury, Berks

Wigney, Frederick (1885) *The Past and the Present.* MS.

Wigney, Frederick (1885) *The Crisis of 1885 in South Australia: Its Cause, Effect and Remedy.* Frederick Wigney. Printer, publisher and journalist. Currie Street, Adelaide.

Wigney, G.A. (1823) *A Philosophical Treatise on Malting and Brewing.* First edition. G. Verrall, Worthing Press.

Wigney, G.A. (1838) *Elementary Dictionary or Cyclopaediae, for the Use of Maltsters, Brewers, Distillers, Rectifiers, Vinegar Manufacturers, and Others.* (

Wigney, G.A. (1850) *An Introductory Treatise on the Theory and Practice of Malting and Brewing.* Brighton: Frederick Wigney.

Wigney, William (1907) *Account of Visit to London.* MS.

Wigney, William (1923) *The Story of My Life.* MS.

B   *Newspapers and periodicals*

Berkshire Chronicle
Brighton Gazette
Brighton Herald
Bury & Norwich Post
Edinburgh Evening News
Exeter & Plymouth Gazette
Exeter Flying Post
Gentleman's Magazine
Hampshire Chronicle
Huddersfield Chronicle
Huddersfield Journal
Inquirer & Commercial News (Perth, WA)
Leeds Intelligencer
Leeds Mercury
Mechanics Magazine

Morning Chronicle
Mount Alexander Mail (Victoria, Australia)
Nature
Reading Mercury
Saunders' Newsletter
The Spectator
Sussex Advertiser
The Times
Western Times
Worcester Journal

C *Websites*

http://www.ancestry.co.uk
http://www.bandhpast.co.uk
https://familysearch.org/
http://homepage.eircom.net
http://www.mocavo.com
http://www.sjmann.supanet.com
http://www.themeister.co.uk/hindley/wool.

INDEX

Lightning Source UK Ltd.
Milton Keynes UK
UKOW06f2324030917
308484UK00004B/14/P